DEVON AND SOME

MINES

Metalliferous and Associated Minerals 1845-1913

Roger Burt
Peter Waite
Ray Burnley

Published by

The University of Exeter

in association with

The Northern Mine Research Society

1984

Roger Burt

ISBN 0 859 89 201 8

Other Publications in this series

The Derbyshire Mineral Statistics	*1845–1913*
The Yorkshire Mineral Statistics	*1845–1913*
The Cumberland Mineral Statistics	*1845–1913*
The Lancashire and Westmorland Mineral	
Statistics with the Isle of Man	*1845–1913*
The Durham and Northumberland Mineral	
Statistics	*1845–1913*

Printed in Great Britain by A. Wheaton & Co. Ltd., Exeter

CONTENTS

This is the sixth volume in our continuing series of county studies of
metalliferous mining in England and Wales from the mid-nineteenth century
to the First World War. It is the first to be published by the University
of Exeter and begins the coverage of the South West. The series arises
from a project funded by the Social Science Research Council in the
Department of Economic History at Exeter to create a computer based data
bank of material originally published in the annual volumes of *The Mineral
Statistics of the United Kingdom*. We have used the facility of the
computer to re-arrange this material in a mine-by-mine format and this
book, like the earlier volumes for Derbyshire, Yorkshire, Cumberland,
Lancashire, Westmoreland, the Isle of Man and Durham and Northumberland,
has been reproduced directly from the output of a high quality printer.
The data is stored in a form permitting flexible programming for the
internal and cross analysis of the production, ownership, management and
employment series, and readers wishing to make use of the data bank,
through terminals in Exeter or elsewhere on the network, should write to
the Department of Economic History, University of Exeter.

The material presented here is in a very similar form to that which
appeared in the original returns, *with a minimum of editorial adjustment*.
Accordingly, mine names have been adopted and spelt in the same way as
they most commonly occurred in the returns made to the Mining Record
Office by the original owners of the mines; information under the
different headings starts and stops just as it did in the first annual
publications; and problems caused by multiple returns for mines of the
same name *but with no clear and readily apparent connection*, have been
resolved by recording them as seperate numbered entries in these listings,
eg. Winford Nos 1-8. The only important changes and new information that
we have introduced relate to locations. Following the precedent set in
the Yorkshire volume, we have changed the locations given in the original
returns to more appropriate current usage and have added Ordnance Survey
Grid References where known. In general, however, the original data for
the South West was more straightforward and easily usable than that for
the northern counties and posed fewer problems of interpretation.
Nevertheless, the authors would be very pleased to hear of any errors that
may have crept in during these editorial adjustments or of any other major
improvements that might be made so that the data bank can be amended.

INTRODUCTION

I

The Mineral Statistics

The official government collection and publication of details of the
output of the British mineral industry was instituted in the 1840s under
the auspices of the Geological Survey and Museum, directed by Sir Henry
de la Beche. We have discussed the development of the ensuing series of
annual publications, which have continued down to the present day, at some
length elsewhere.[1] It is useful, however, to outline the main stages of
that development. The work was conducted by the Mining Record Office,
which was initially part of the Geological Survey and Museum, and was
effectively the responsibility of Robert Hunt, Keeper of the Mining
Records. The first published series, relating to the output of copper and
lead, principally in the years 1845 to 1847, appeared in *Memoirs of the
Geological Survey of Great Britain and the Museum of Practical Geology in
London* Vols.I and II, (H.M.S.O. 1845 and 1847). This was regarded at the
time as a limited exercise and no commitment was made for the publication
of further annual series. In 1853, however, Hunt took the opportunity to
update and extend these earlier series in a volume published by the
Geological Survey, under his name, entitled *Records of the School of Mines
and of Science Applied to the Arts*, Vol. I Pt IV. In that same year a
Treasury Committee inquiring into the working of the Geological Survey and
Museum reported favourably on the activities of the Mining Record Office
and recommended that its activities should be placed, 'on a more regular
footing'. This signalled the beginning of the regular collection and
publication of a widening range of data relating to mineral extraction and
related manufacturing and transportation.
    The first of the new annual series, published under the title *Memoirs
of the Geological Survey of Great Britain and of the Museum of Practical
Geology: Mining Records: The Mineral Statistics of the United Kingdom of
Great Britain and Ireland*, appeared in 1855 and was for the year 1853, so
continuing an unbroken run for some production data, eg lead and copper,
from 1845. Thereafter the volumes were published by the Geological Survey
in unbroken series until 1882, usually appearing in the autumn of the year
following the record year. Robert Hunt retired following the preparation
of the 1881 volume and the opportunity was taken to reorganise and
consolidate the now considerably expanded range of data collection. This
was done by transferring the Mining Record Office from the Museum of
Practical Geology to the Home Office, where the Mine Inspectors,

---

1   See R.Burt and P.Waite, "An Introduction to the Mineral Statistics of
    the United Kingdom" Northern Mine Research Society, British Mining
    No 23 (1983) 40-58

established by the *Coal Mine Inspection Act* of 1850, had for many years been publishing a similar range of output data in their annual reports. In particular, the *Coal and Metalliferous Mines Regulation Acts* of 1872 had required all active mines in the country to furnish the Mines Inspectorate with details of their output and employment and it was thought wasteful to continue the collection of voluntary returns and computations of the Mining Record Office alongside these.

The first of the new series, which was prepared by Hunt's old staff and closely followed the format of the earlier publications, appeared in 1884 under the title *The Mining and Mineral Statistics of the United Kingdom of Great Britain and Ireland for 1882* and was produced, unlike its earlier counterparts, as a Parliamentary Paper. The following year the title changed again to *Summaries of the Reports of the Inspectors of Mines to Her Majesty's Secretary of State, and the Mineral Statistics of the United Kingdom of Great Britain and Ireland, including Lists of Mines and Mineral Works* and for the years 1884 to 1887 inclusive they appeared annually as *The Mineral and Mining Statistics of The United Kingdom of Great Britain and Ireland, including Lists of Mines and Mineral Worked.* During these years the volumes included returns of a) the quantity and value of all minerals wrought b) the numbers of people employed in and about the mines and open works c) the number of fatal accidents in the mines d) a list of the mine owners, managers and agents e) a list of the recorded plans of abandoned mines that had been deposited at the Home Office f) an appendix showing the production of minerals in the British colonies and possessions.

From 1888 to 1896 the returns appeared as *The Mineral Statistics of the United Kingdom of Great Britain and Ireland with the Isle of Man* and this time the change in title was accompanied by important changes in the content. The details of accidents in the mines, previously held over from the early annual reports of the Inspectors of Mines, were dropped for separate publication, as was *The List of Mines*, a regular appendix of the names of the mine owners, agents, managers and numbers employed, which had been included at the back of *The Mineral Statistics* since 1853 for coal mines, 1859 for most metalliferous mines and 1863 for Iron mines. Finally in 1897 the title and content of the annual returns were changed to a format that they were to keep through to the First World War. For that year the volume appeared under the general title *Mines and Quarries: General Report and Statistics*. It was divided into four separate sections, Part III containing details of output and being subtitled *General Report and Statistics Relating to the Output and Value of the Mineral Raised in the United Kingdom, the Amount and Value of the Metals Produced and the Exports and Imports of Minerals.*

It is notable that until 1897 the 'Clerks of the Mineral Statistics', who had responsibility for preparing the publications, were still largely the same men that had worked with Robert Hunt from the earliest days of the Mining Record Office. This provided a strong element of continuity and an unparalleled wealth of experience in collecting and editing the material. Following Hunt's retirement in 1882, the new Home Office department had been jointly run by Richard Meade and James B.Jordan. Meade had originally been appointed by Hunt as early as 1841 and had been joined by Jordan in 1858. Meade retired from the Home Office in 1889 but Jordan continued until 1897, so consolidating a period of more than half a century's data gathering under three close associates.

II

Devon and Somerset Mineral Production

The mining of metals was an important part of the regional economy of Devon and Somerset for more than a thousand years. For most of that time the mines of this region were among the largest and richest producers in the country. By the middle of the nineteenth century, however, the prosperous years were already long in the past. A handfull of large mines kept Devon in the forefront of copper and manganese production but most of the tin deposits - its traditional staple - had been exhausted. Similarly, the once highly productive lead mines of the Mendips were long past their peak and most remaining activity was concerned with the reworking of old tips. Like the ancient lead districts of the Derbyshire Peak, mining in both counties had substantially reverted to small scale, poorly capitalised ventures, picking over the leavings of earlier generations.[2] Only a few mines working recently discovered deposits continued to carry the flag of modern large scale mining. Finally, in the twentieth century, increasing competition, low prices and the further impoverishment of the lodes led to the final demise of metal mining activity in the district.

The production of *tin* in Devon and Somerset was confined to mines in the immediate vicinity of Dartmoor and was traditionally organised under the stannary system. When records of production first began to be regularly collected by the Mining Record Office in the 1850s, total output from the district rarely amounted to more than 200 tons a year and it contributed only 2 per cent of national production. By the last quarter of the century, this had fallen to usually far less than 100 tons a year and was only a tiny fraction of total output. See Table 1. Taking the period 1854 to 1913 as a whole there were 66 mines producing tin in Devon, with a total output of 5,758 tons of dressed ore, valued at £394,740. Of these mines, 50 had a total output of less than 100 tons each and only four produced more than 400 tons; viz. Birch Tor and Vitifer, Wheal Sidney, Mary Hutchings and Yeoland Consols. Birch Tor and Vitifer was easily the most productive of these, with a total output of 1,266 tons of dressed ore, valued at £87,847. Working continued on this site through to the 1920s but even this mine hardly ranked as a medium sized producer compared with its larger and deeper Cornish neighbours.[3]

The Somerset equivalent of Dartmoor tin was the equally long established *lead* industry of the Mendip hills. As J.W.Gough has shown,

---

2 See R.Burt and M.Atkinson "The Mineral Statistics and Derbyshire Mining" *Bulletin of the Peak District Mines Historical Society* Vol 6 No 3 April 1976

3 See D.G.Broughton, "The Birch Tor and Vitifer Mining Complex" *Transactions of the Cornish Institute of Engineers* Vol XXIV (1968-69) 25-49 and M.Atkinson with R.Burt and P.Waite,*Dartmoor Mines:The Mines of the Granite Mass* (Exeter Industrial Archaeology Group, Exeter, 1978)

the mines of this district had been major suppliers of national and international markets down to the early eighteenth century but by the early nineteenth century they were virtually exhausted.[4] By the 1850s, the small remaining lead output from Somerset was derived almost exclusively from the reprocessing of old waste tips — an activity made economic by the development of new and improved methods of ore dressing and smelting that enabled the recovery of small traces of ore abandoned by the "old men". In the annual *Mineral Statistics* this production was returned as an estimated total for the Mendips as a whole or, briefly, in the early 1890s, under the heading "St.Cuthbert's Lead Works".

From the second quarter of the nineteenth century, Somerset lead production was augmented by an increasing output from new and revived mines in Devon. These were located mainly in the Teign and Tamar valleys. Between the mid–1840s and the late 1850s, Devon lead production more than doubled and although falling off slightly in the 1860s, remained at a fairly high level through to the early 1870s. The two counties together reached a maximum share of national output in 1854 with nearly five per cent of the total; a small but significant level. See Table 2. The Devon mines made a much greater contribution, however, in terms of their abnormally high silver content. During the peak years of lead production in the mid–1850s they produced a by-product of over 100,000 oz of silver annually, which accounted for more than 20 per cent of total U.K. silver output. See Table 3. Taken together, there were 48 mines producing lead in Devon during years between 1845 and 1913, of which 37 were also silver producers. Like the tin mines, most of these were small operations, with 28 ventures having a total output of less than 100 tons of lead/silver ore each. However, 12 mines produced over 500 tons of lead/silver ore and eight of these had an output in excess of 1,000 tons. The eight largest mines had a total production of 56,042 tons of argentiferous ore, which was equal to nearly 89 percent of all Devon output. Three mines were clear leaders — Frankmills, Wheal Tamar and Wheal Exmouth, in that order — and their combined production amounted to nearly two thirds of Devon output. Since the silver content of the ores was not given for all years, it is impossible to break down the structure of that production for the period as a whole. However, during the years 1859 to 1861, seven of the eight leading lead mines were responsible for 99 per cent of silver output. The Tamar mines were the largest producers usefully supported by Wheal Exmouth and Frankmills in that order. By far the single richest silver mine was Tamar Silver Lead. In 1859 it produced 40,959 oz of silver, equivalent to over 60 per cent of Devon's total output for the year. This was derived from only 842 tons of dressed lead ore, giving a silver content of 48.6 oz per ton — among the richest in the British Isles.[5]

After the mid–1870s the Devon lead and silver mines went into a sharp decline and within ten years the industry was completely at a standstill.[6] The small remaining output of the two counties was derived exclusively from the reworking of Somerset waste heaps, which produced a few hundred tons of lead annually but no significant silver production. See Tables 2 and 3.

---

4   J.W.Gough, *Mines of Mendip* (Oxford, 1930)
5   See F.Booker, *The Industrial Archaeology of the Tamar Valley* (Newton Abbot, David and Charles, 1967)
6   See C.J.Schmitz, *The Teign Valley Silver-Lead Mines 1806 - 1880* (Northern Mines Research Society, British Mining No 15, 1980)

With the decline of lead and silver production, mining speculators in the Teign valley turned their attention to the exploitation of associated deposits of *barytes*. Used in the manufacture of paint and various other industrial processes,[7] this mineral was produced from Frankmills and, on a larger scale, from the Teign Valley mine at Bridford. See Table 4.[8] Similarly, the exhausted Tamar lead mines turned to the production of *fluorspar*, which was experiencing a rapidly increasing demand as a flux for iron smelting. An output of up to several hundred tons of fluorspar a year was achieved at Tamar Valley and Tamar Silver Lead in the late 1870s and early 1880s and Wheal Bedford and Frankmills also produced small quantities. Somerset mines also produced some barytes and fluorspar but with the exception of Winford this was never returned on a mine—by—mine basis. See Table 5.

Zinc was produced in small quantities at eight mines in Devon during the nineteenth century. At five of them it was as a by—product of lead mining and at two a by—product of copper.Only one – Silver Brook – could be properly described as a zinc mine but that also had a small by—product of lead. Of the 4,273 tons of zinc ore produced in the county between 1856 and 1873, 1,795 tons came from Silver Brook, 1,558 tons from Wheal Exmouth, 477 tons from Collacomb and 160 tons from Wheal Friendship – the latter two mines being primarily copper producers. These four mines together produced over 93 per cent of Devon's output of zinc during the period, though by national standards they were small producers, accounting for only just over one per cent of U.K. output. See Table 6. There was no recorded output of zinc from Somerset mines in the period between the mid—nineteenth century and the First World War, though the county had previously been a major producer.

While tin and lead ran out and the few surviving ventures used their ingenuity in the production of by—products such as barytes, fluorspar and zinc to supplement their dwindling income, the mining of *copper* kept Devon firmly in the national eye. The total U.K. output of copper ore increased by more than 50 per cent during the 1850s, while Devon's production more than doubled during the first half of that decade alone. This increased the county's share of the total from less than seven per cent in 1845 to over 17 percent in 1857. Copper was booming and new Devon mines, mainly in and around the Tamar Valley, were exploiting the rising market. Production remained high through the early 1860s but prices then began to decline sharply with rapidly increasing imports. The average price of best copper, which had been over £100 per ton during the 1850s and early 1860s, fell by more than a quarter to £72 per ton in 1870 and total U.K. output was more than halved in just six years. The industry had seen a sudden and permanent reversal in its fortunes. Even the rich and profitable Devon mines felt the pinch and their production began to fall off. However, they generally held up much better than their older Cornish competitors and by the early 1870s Devon's share of total domestic production had risen to almost 25 percent. Thereafter the story remained essentially the same through to the early 1890s. By 1886 the average price of best copper had fallen to £44 per ton and national ouput to 18,617 tons – less than eight percent of its high 1859 level. Devon

7   See R.Burt, "Minor to Major Minerals" *Geology Teaching* Vol No 1984
8   See C.J.Schmitz,"The Early Growth of The Devon Barytes Industry 1835 – 1875" and "The Development and Decline of The Devon Barytes Industry 1875 – 1958" *Transactions of the Devonshire Association* Vol 106 (1974) 59—76 and Vol 109 (1977) 117—134

production had also fallen off to just a quarter of its earlier peak level but now accounted for over half of national output. At this point prices generally stabilized at the new lower level but profits had virtually disappeared and production continued its decline everywhere through to 1893. Devon's share of the total slipped slightly but generally remained well above 40 percent. See Table 7. By this time, however, only a small rump of the once great industry survived in Britain and the remaining copper production had now become essentially the by-product of other mining operations - mainly tin and arsenic. In Devon, for example, over 93 percent of copper production in 1893 came from Devon Great Consols but the copper output of that mine accounted for less than 10 percent of total sales — most of its income being derived from the production of arsenic. Accordingly, copper production began to fluctuate, not with changes in the copper market, but with changes in the demand for these other products. When the demand for arsenic tailed off sharply in the early years of the new century, Devon Great Consols closed and with the exception of a very few small producers, Devon copper production came virtually to an end in the years preceeding the First World War. There was no production of copper in Somerset during this period.

As might be expected, the structure of the copper mining sector of the industry was noticably different from that of tin and lead. Firstly, there were far fewer small producers — only 17 mines out of the total of 78, produced less than 100 tons of ore, while 39 produced over 1,000 tons. Not only was there a larger than usual number of medium sized mines but also there were 12 large producers, with a total output in excess of 10,000 tons. As was common elsewhere, however, a small group of the very largest producers heavily dominated the industry. The five largest mines — Devon Great Consols, Bedford United, Wheal Maria, Wheal Friendship and Wheal Crebor - all with a total output of copper ore in excess of 30,000 tons, accounted for 81 per cent of Devon production during the period. Just one of these mines, Devon Great Consols, which also came to include Wheal Maria and West Maria, produced over two thirds of the county's on its own. Other large mines, like Bedford United and Wheal Friendship, which could themselvs be counted among Britain's biggest producers, were completely overshadowed by the massive three quarters of a million tons of copper ore extracted from the Devon Great Consols set, principally during the 1840s, 1850s and 1860s. During the 1850s it was probably the largest copper producer anywhere in the world and even during the depressed and declining 1880s it remained easily the most productive mine in Britain, accounting for nearly 30 per cent of domestic output between 1885 and 1890. In no other industry has Devon ever had such a large and internationally recognised enterprise.

The continued success and importance of Devon Great Consols as a copper producer was made possible entirely by its capacity to expand its earnings from the production and sale of a jointly occuring mineral - arsenic. The calcining of arsenic at the mine was rapidly and continuously expanded through the late 1860s and 1870s and became its principal source of income from 1879, with copper being effectively relegated to the subsidiary role of a by-product. Although it experienced strong competition from several other major producers in Devon and Cornwall, who also attempted to capitalise on the bouyant American demand during the last quarter of the century, this great mine again dominated the field as easily the largest producer. Between 1870 and 1900 it accounted for over 43 per cent of the total domestic output of arsenic and was primarily responsible for making Devon as a whole the source of well over half the annual U.K. production throughout the last quarter of the nineteenth century. When Devon Great Consols stopped working in 1904, the county's output immediately fell to only just over 10 per cent of domestic production. See Table 8. Although the history of the mine has been admirably sketched by J.C.Goodridge and others,[9] it clearly warrants more detailed study and would support a monograph of its own, similar to those already published on several major Cornish copper and tin mines.

While acknowledging the importance of Devon Great Consols, its dominance should not be permitted to disguise the large quantities of arsenic derived from several other major Devon mines and the important contribution which it made to their total income and survival. Some mines calcined the ore themselvs to produce refined arsenc, occasionally selling surplus ore to other mines with spare refining capacity, while others chose to sell all of their ore in the form of unprocessed arsenical pyrite. See Table 8. A total of 29 Devon mines made returns of arsenic and/or arsenical pyrite sales during the late nineteenth and early twentieth centuries, most of them producing it as a joint or by-product of copper and a few of tin. The biggest producers were the large copper mines, particularly Gawton, Wheal Friendship and Wheal Crebor, in that order. Between the early 1870s and 1902, Gawton sold arsenic and arsenical pyrites to a total value of £184,627, almost three and a half times the value of its copper output during the same period, and it made the transition to becoming primarily an arsenic mine around 1880. It was the third largest arsenic producer in Britain, behind Devon Great Consols and East Pool and Agar. Wheal Friendship, the third largest Devon arsenic producer and the seventh in the national ranking, sold a total of £64,099 worth of arsenic and arsenical pyrites, mainly from the mid-1870s. This ammounted to less than a quarter of its total revenue from copper sales during the period but arsenic production did become the major source of income after 1874. Taking these two mines together with Devon Great Consols, it is quite clear that the survival of the great bulk of Devon copper production during the closing decades of the nineteenth century was entirely due to the primary incentive of marketing arsenic. Again, there was no production of arsenic in Somerset.

Devon's position as a major international producer of silver, copper, and arsenic was complemented by its role as one of the most important domestic sources of *manganese*. Like the other major minerals, this was largely because the most productive lodes did not begin to be exploited until the late eighteenth and early nineteenth centuries and accordingly the mid-nineteenth century encompassed the years of their main exploitation. The production of managanese in the county started in the Upton Pyne and Newton St Cyres areas just to the north west of Exeter and these became the leading producers in England and possibly Europe in the decades around 1800. By the mid-nineteenth century, however, the centre of production had shifted to the Teign valley and, more importantly, the Milton Abbot/Marystow district of West Devon. Through the 1850s, 1860s and early 1870s these mines were virtually the only source of domestic production and competed well with rapidly increasing imports of foreign

---

9   J.C.Goodridge,"Devon Great Consols: A Study of Victorian Mining
     Enterprise" *Transactions of the Devonshire Association* Vol 96 (1964)
     228-268; R.Shambrook, "The Devon Great Consolidated Copper Mining
     Company" and J.Brooke, "The Last Years of Devon Great Consols" both in
     the *Journal of the Trevithick Society* No9 (1982) 62-68 and 69-72.

ore. Thereafter, however, their production began to fall off and although they were still responsible for over three quarters of U.K. output in the mid-1880s, the sudden rise of new mines in Merioneth and later Caernarvonshire sharply reduced their contribution to just over one per cent by the end of that decade. With markedly lower prices output from the important Chillaton and Hogstor mine was severely curtailed and Devon production never again exceeded more than a few hundred tons annually. For the rest of the century its share of domestic production fluctuated, quite signicantly, with changes in the output of the North Wales mines.[10] During these years, the rapidly rising domestic demand for manganese – which was mainly used as an additive to control oxygenation in steel production – was met by a great increase in imports. In 1880 these had stood at only just over 16,000 tons a year but by 1899 they had reached over a quarter of a million tons and by the end of the first decade of the new century this figure had again been more than doubled. See Table 9.

There were 25 mines in Devon producing manganese during the late nineteenth and early twentieth centuries of which the great majority were very small producers: 16 had a total output of less than 100 tons of ore and six produced between 100 and 500 tons. Just three very large mines were responsible for 93 per cent of the county's total production: Newton St Cyres, seeing revived working in the 1870s; Monkston, in the new Milton Abbot/ Brentor district, which achieved high levels of output in the 1880s; and Chillerton and Hogstor, clearly the largest producer during the period, with a total output of 53,014 tons of ore valued at nearly a quarter of a million pounds. Its production alone was equal to more than 85 percent of total Devon output and during its peak years in the early 1870s it accounted for around 99 per cent of domestic production. In 1873 it supplied nearly one quarter of the estimated domestic consumption of manganese in the U.K. Although never a particularly large mine and not conducted on the same scale as the great copper and arsenic enterprises, it was a very close rival to Devon Great Consols in terms of its relative contribution to the total supply and consumption of its major product. In Somerset there was some very small scale working of manganese at three mines in the Brendon hills but in total it amounted to no more than a few hundred tons. Most of the output came from Rose mine in the early 1880s.[11] However, it should be noticed that the spathose iron ores of the Brendon hills were also relatively rich in manganese. The manganese was never separated and sold as such but the manganiferous ores were used for very similar purposesin the iron and steel industry. If that "unseparated" production is taken into account, the total manganese output of Somerset would probably exceed even that of Devon.[12]

Finally, attention may be turned from non-ferrous to ferrous mining. *Iron* was principally produced in three areas in the two counties: the

---

10 C.G.Down, *The Manganese Mines of North Wales* (Northern Mine Research Society, British Mining No 14, 1980)

11 For a detailed survey of manganese mining in Devon, Somerset and Cornwall see I.Wilkie and R.Burt, "Manganese Mining in the South West of England" *Journal of the Trevithick Society* No 11 1984

12 For a discussion of the nature and uses of manganiferous iron ores, see M.Atkinson, "Iron Ore Mining in Mainland Britain in the Nineteenth and Early Twentieth Centuries and its Links with the Iron and Steel Industry, with Particular Reference to Cleveland, Cumbria and the South Western Counties of England" 2 Vols (University of Exeter PhD Thesis, 1981)

Brixham and Ilsington district of south Devon; around North Molton in
north Devon; and, most importantly, the Brendon hills in Somerset. It was
the only mineral to be produced in greater quantities in Somerset than
Devon during the period, with a production of 902,781 tons compared with
341,354 tons. In terms of the total output of ore it was clearly the most
important mining activity in the area, with a total output of nearly one
and a quarter million tons of ore compared with just over one million tons
of copper. By value, however, iron ranked a long way behind copper but
was probably more valuable than the total output of tin, lead and silver.

Like copper, manganese and lead, the development of iron mining in
Devon and Somerset began in the late eighteenth century and gradually
developed, mainly in the south Devon area, during the early nineteenth
century. A number of small but high quality deposits were exploited,
including magnetite and brown, red, specular and micaceous haematite. The
absence of cheap local supplies of coal meant that this ore had to be
shipped out of the district for smelting and processing, most of it to
South Wales. With these established links, it was not surprising that
when, in the mid-nineteenth century, the iron masters of that district
began to find difficulties in meeting their ore requirements from local
mines, they should turn their attention across the Bristol channel in the
hope of finding large new deposits of ore. The rich spathose and
haematite deposits of north Devon and Somerset appeared particularly
promising, offering substantial reserves of ores that were especially
useful in controlling the quality of finished railway iron, which was the
main and most rapidly growing product of the Welsh iron industry.
Companies like the Ebbw Vale Steel, Iron and Coal Company made major
investments in developing mines in the Brendon hills and output increased
rapidly throughthe 1850s, 1860s and 1870s. However, they never achieved
the very high volume production that had been hoped for, largely because
production and transportation costs remained high.[13] The total annual
output of Devon and Somerset iron mines never amounted to more than six
per cent of the national total and was generally much less than one per
cent. See Table 10. When imports of cheap foreign ore began to rapidly
increase from the beginning of the last quarter of the century, the
Brendon hills mines, like most other metal mines in the south west, went
into sharp decline. By the end of the century their combined output
amounted to no more than a few thousand tons annually.

The north and south Devon mines also had their heyday before the
mid-1880s, with the largest mines - Brixham, Florence and Haytor - seeing
their most productive years in the 1860s, 1870s, or early 1880s. The
prosperous conditions and relatively high prices of those years also
encouraged some non-ferrous mines, such as Bampfylde copper mine and
Frankmills lead mine, to experiment with the extraction and separation of
iron ores, sometimes with considerable success. Similarly, Molland found
new life as an iron mine in the 1870s after a previous existence as a
copper producer. Although the last years of the century saw a reversal of
these fortunes almost everywhere, several mines continued to produce quite
large quantities of ore in to the first decade of the new century.
Brimley and Molland, for example, had an output of several thousand tons

13 See M.Atkinson, P.Waite and R.Burt, "The Iron Mining Industry in
    Devon" Northern Mine Research Society, British Mining No 19 (1980-82)
    27-33 and D.G.Dixon, "Mining and the Community in the Parishes of
    North Molton, South Molton, Molland and Twitchen, Devonshire"
    (University of Southampton M.Phil Thesis, 1983)

of ore each in some years during the late 1890s and 1900s. The most steady and sustained record of production, however, was at the small but very specialised micaceous haematite mines, located just to the north of Bovey Tracy; ie Great Rock, Hawkmoor, Hennock, Kelly, Plumley and Shuttamoor. Several of these mines worked fairly continuously throughout the late nineteenth and much of the early twentieth century.[14] They produced small quantities of an ore which commanded a comparatively high price for use in a crude, unsmelted form in the manufacture of paint.[15] Some of the production returns for these mines had to be extracted from the *Mineral Statistics* listings for ochre and umber, where they had been mistakenly recorded by the Mining Record Office.

In this brief look at the scale and structure of mining in Devon and Somerset, attention has been mainly focused on the production employment data, though starting at a much later date, reflects a very similar story — that of a few very large employers and a multiplicity of small operations. For those employed in mining, this represented a great diversity of work experience and conditions. Some, such as those employed at Devon Great Consols, were part of a regular, large-scale work force, employed in deep mining and achieving high levels of productivity. Others, like those working at East Vitifer, were often no more than a handful of semi-independent workers scratching a living from a poor near-surface deposit. While the work experience of those employed at Devon Great Consols was that of one of the country's largest, modern disciplined industrial labour forces, that of the smaller mines was still essentially part of an ancient pre-industrial tradition. Similarly, the ownership and management material reflects the role of new systems of joint stock limited liability company organisation in developing major new mines, like Devon Great Consols, and preserving old declining workings, like Wheal Friendship. At the same time traditional private or small partnership operations continued at the marginal ventures. It should be noticed, however, that many of the larger and more successful mines continued through into the last quarter of the century on the basis of restricted small partnership finance, eg. Chillaton and Hogstor. This was largely because several of the families involved in these ventures — such as the Sims and Williams — had longstanding links with the industry throughout the South West and brought considerable experience, expertise and capital to their enterprises. Much still remains to be done on the role of labour, capital and management in the structure and efficiency of British metal mining and it is hoped that the material published here will assist in that research.

---

14 See M.Atkinson and C.Schmitz, "Kelly Iron Mine, near Bovey Tracy" *Devon Historian* Vol II (Oct 1975) 27-34
15 See F.B.Mitchell, "Mineral Pigments"*Mine and Quarry Engineering*(Nov 1944) 277-9 and (Jan 1945) 9-14

III

The Mine Tables

The information which appears in the following tables is the same as that published in the annual editions of the *Mineral Statistics*, now re-arranged in a mine-by-mine format. Some editorial judgement has been exercised in re-compiling the material, in order to link returns together and provide for necessary cross-referencing, but wherever possible the mine names, production record, ownership, management, employment and even comments are given just as they appeared in the original. If any catagory of information is missing under a mine name, or if the series cover only a few years, or indeed if an entire entry is not included, it is because there were no returns in the *Mineral Statistics*. In order to facilitate the alphabetical arrangement of the material, we have omitted the common prefix "Wheal" from mine names.

A problem that has occured in earlier volumes in this series but which has been particularly apparent here, is that of the random transfer of returns for some mines between neighbouring counties. The original *Mineral Statistics* incorrectly located some of the production returns for 20 Cornish mines in Devon and approximately seven Devon mines in Cornwall. Similarly the original Somerset data included returns for three Devon mines and the Devon data included returns for one Somerset mine. Three other entries in the Devon listings appear to have been "strays" from more distant areas. The totals for the counties concerned were accordingly distorted by these errors. In the past we have sometimes tried to correct these problems by transfering the relevant material between counties but here, in the interests of the faithful reproduction of the original and acknowledging the possibility of our own error, we have left them unchanged. We have, however, attempted to indicate the relevant entries in the text and they are as follows:

Cornish Mines incorrectly located in the Devon returns

Arthur	Martha, Great
Atway	" , West
Calstock Consols	Mary Great Consols
Drakewalls	New Consols
Emmens United	New Great Consols
Friendship & Prosper	Pawton
Gunnislake	Polharman
" , East	Prince of Wales
" , Old	Richards Friendship
Laddock	Toy Tor

Devon mines incorrectly located in the Cornwall returns

Adams	Haytor
Devon & Cornwall United	Langstone
Friendship, North	Whitleigh
Girt Down	

Somerset mines incorrectly located in the Devon returns

    Exmoor

Devon mines incorrectly located in the Somerset returns

    Fullabrook   Furze Hill
    Parracombe

"Stray" mines from other districts incorrectly located
in the Devon returns

    Maex, South (Manx, South Isle of Man)
    Thomas United (Cardiganshire)
    True Blue (Denbighshire)

Not all entries for all of these mines were wrongly located. Some of their returns were under the correct county. One particular problem arose for South Bedford and East Gunnislake which were worked for a long time as one mine, staddling the river Tamar border between Devon and Cornwall. The ownership returns appeared in the Devon listings but production was given in different years under both counties.

The only new material that has been added to the *Mine Tables* is some additional cross-referencing information, the adjustment of some locations for current usage, and Ordnance Survey Grid Reference figures. The Grid References have been derived from our own research, checked against J.V.Ramsden, "Notes on the Mines of Devonshire" *Transactions of the Devonshire Association* Vol LXXXIV (1952–3) 81–104; A.K.Hamilton Jenkin,*The Mines of Devon* Vol 1 The Southern Area (Newton Abbot, David and Charles, 1974) and Vol 2 North and East of Dartmoor (Exeter, Devon Library Services, 1981); H.Harris,*The Industrial Archaeology of Dartmoor* (Newton Abbot, David and Charles, 1968); P.F.Claughton, "The Metalliferous Mines of North Devon and Exmoor" *Plymouth Mineral and Mining Club* Vol 4 No 1 Spring 1973 4–9 and Vol 5 No 1 Sping 1974 9–10; and F.J.Rottenbury, "Geology, Mineralogy and Mining History of the Metalliferous Mining Areas of Exmoor" (University of Leeds PhD Thesis, 1974). The exact location of the iron mines of the Brixham/Torbay area proved to be an intractable problem. This was largely because the companies which raised the ore appear to have left very few records and the area concerned has since been heavily redeveloped. We would like to thank Justin Brooke for his help and advice on several of these matters.

Four principal categories of information are included for every mine, where they are available. *Production* data is given by type of mineral produced and often includes ore output, metal content, and value – the latter sometimes being calculated by assay and average market price. The absence of detailed production returns under a particular mine name should not necessarily be taken to imply that the mine was not working in those years, since its output might be disguised in the county aggregate figures, sundries or joint returns listed under other mines. Wherever possible we have tried to indicate such listings through cross references in the *Comment* section. In this volume, the *Comment* section for iron mines has been used to indicate the types of ore being produced. This was commonly brown haematite(BH), red haematite(RH), micaceous haematite(MH), haematite(HE), spathose(SP) and magnetite(MO). Similarly, it has sometimes been possible to use the copper production comment section to indicate the method of sale of that ore; the sales being at the Cornish ticketings(C), the Swansea ticketings(S), or private contract(P). The returns for the production of the different minerals on a mine-by-mine basis began to appear from different dates: lead from 1845; copper from 1848; tin and silver from 1852; zinc from 1854; arsenic and barytes from 1855; iron and manganese from 1858 and fluorspar from 1874. In the early years there was undoubtedly some under recording and the number of the mines included in the annual listings usually increased noticeably during the first few years of recording.[16]

Ownership and *Management* returns often give a good indication of the years of activity at a mine, though drawn from *The List of Mines*, appended to the back of the early *Mineral Statistics*, they are not available for non-ferrous mines before 1859 or iron mines before 1863. These annual *Lists* were said to include the names and addresses of the owners and agents of all mines that were working during the year. However, careful examination of them reveals that major revisions were periodically conducted when unusually large numbers of mines suddenly disappeared. This suggests that they were not carefully edited for every edition and that they therefore continued to include some mines long after they had been abandoned. The *Employment* returns were also drawn from the *List of Mines* and provide a further check on the periods, level and type of activity at the mines. For example, a prospecting or developing working might show significant levels of employment even though there was little or no production or sales of ore. Similarly, a changing distribution of workers between underground and surface operations can give an idea of when ventures began to run down their mining operations and concentrate only on the redressing of spoil heaps. It should be remembered that many of the smaller mines at best provided only part-time employment for their labour force and that the same miners may have been counted several times over at different workings. Unfortunately, the decision to publish detailed employment returns appears to have been left to the discretion of the local Mine Inspectors and while this began for some non-ferrous mines in Devon at the relatively early date of 1878, in Somerset it did not start until 1883 and thereafter it is difficult to decide whether they are continuous and inclusive.

---

16 See R.Burt, "The Mineral Statistics of the United Kingdom: An Analysis of the Accuracy of the Copper and Tin Returns for Cornwall and Devon" *Journal of the Trevithick Society* No 8 (1981) 31-46

Table 1

Devon and Somerset Tin ore production and its share
of total U.K. output 1852 to 1913

Year	D'n & S't Ore(tons)	U.K. Ore(tons)	% of UK Ore Prod	Year	D'n & S't Ore(tons)	U.K. Ore(tons)	% of UK Ore Prod
1852	177	9,674	1.83	1883	70	14,469	0.48
1853	279	8,866	3.15	1884	26	15,117	0.18
1854	232	8,747	2.65	1885	53	14,377	0.37
1855	180	8,947	2.02	1886	107	14,232	0.76
1856	136	9,243	1.48	1887	106	14,189	0.75
1857	95	9,709	0.98	1888	88	14,370	0.61
1858	54	9,960	0.55	1889	53	13,809	0.39
1859	111	10,180	1.09	1890	43	14,911	0.29
1860	175	10,400	1.68	1891	44	14,488	0.31
1861	238	10,963	2.17	1892	96	14,357	0.67
1862	203	11,841	1.72	1893	52	13,699	0.38
1863	282	14,225	1.99	1894	30	12,910	0.23
1864	307	13,985	2.20	1895	29	10,612	0.28
1865	255	14,123	1.81	1896	6	7,663	0.08
1866	184	13,785	1.34	1897	–	7,120	0.01
1867	78	11,067	0.71	1898	1	7,380	0.02
1868	54	11,584	0.47	1899	3	6,392	0.05
1869	127	13,884	0.92	1900	8	6,801	0.12
1870	44	15,235	0.29	1901	8	7,288	0.12
1871	139	16,898	0.82	1902	8	7,560	0.11
1872	134	13,381	1.01	1903	28	7,382	0.38
1873	93	14,838	0.63	1904	9	6,742	0.13
1874	129	13,762	0.94	1905	27	7,201	0.37
1875	135	14,005	0.96	1906	39	7,154	0.55
1876	47	13,649	0.35	1907	93	7,080	1.32
1877	21	14,092	0.15	1908	192	8,008	2.40
1878	47	15,124	0.31	1909	123	8,289	1.48
1879	32	14,280	0.22	1910	89	7,572	1.18
1880	32	13,376	0.25	1911	80	7,746	1.04
1881	15	12,898	0.12	1912	101	8,166	1.25
1882	50	14,045	0.36	1913	97	8,355	1.17
				Total	5,818	702,205	0.83

All tin production came from Devon mines

Table 2

Devon and Somerset Lead ore production and its share
of total U.K. output 1845 to 1913

Year	D'n & S't Ore(tons)	U.K. Ore(tons)	% of UK Ore Prod	Year	D'n & S't Ore(tons)	U.K. Ore(tons)	% of UK Ore Prod
1845	1,983	78,267	2.53	1880	504	72,245	0.70
1846	1,604	74,551	2.15	1881	374	64,702	0.58
1847	1,721	83,747	2.05	1882	289	65,002	0.44
1848	1,375	78,944	1.74	1883	491	50,980	0.96
1849	2,055	86,823	2.37	1884	666	54,485	1.22
1850	2,332	92,958	2.51	1885	3	51,302	0.01
1851	2,551	92,312	2.76	1886	20	53,420	0.04
1852	3,077	91,198	3.37	1887	–	51,563	0.00
1853	3,014	85,043	3.54	1888	–	51,259	0.00
1854	4,140	90,554	4.57	1889	–	48,465	0.00
1855	4,036	92,038	4.39	1890	182	45,651	0.40
1856	3,888	101,998	3.81	1891	80	43,859	0.18
1857	3,076	96,820	3.18	1892	108	40,024	0.27
1858	3,779	95,856	3.94	1893	480	40,808	1.18
1859	4,022	91,382	4.40	1894	691	40,599	1.70
1860	3,819	88,791	4.30	1895	–	38,412	0.00
1861	3,623	90,666	4.00	1896	–	41,069	0.00
1862	2,829	95,312	2.97	1897	229	35,338	0.65
1863	2,278	91,283	2.50	1898	268	32,985	0.81
1864	4,030	94,463	4.27	1899	–	30,999	0.00
1865	2,898	90,452	3.20	1900	–	32,010	0.00
1866	1,855	91,048	2.04	1901	1,000	27,976	3.57
1867	1,687	93,432	1.81	1902	984	24,606	4.00
1868	2,658	95,236	2.79	1903	200	26,567	0.75
1869	2,618	96,866	2.70	1904	–	26,374	0.00
1870	2,572	98,177	2.62	1905	134	27,649	0.48
1871	2,829	93,965	3.01	1906	350	30,795	1.14
1872	2,068	81,619	2.53	1907	936	32,533	2.88
1873	1,429	73,500	1.94	1908	576	29,249	1.97
1874	1,931	76,202	2.53	1909	–	29,744	0.00
1875	1,881	77,746	2.42	1910	–	28,534	0.00
1876	1,016	79,096	1.28	1911	–	23,910	0.00
1877	790	80,850	0.98	1912	–	25,409	0.00
1878	773	77,351	1.00	1913	–	24,282	0.00
1879	404	66,877	0.60				
				Total	95,206	4,408,228	2.16

After 1890 all lead production came from Somerset mines.

Table 3: Devon and Somerset Silver ore production and its
share of total U.K. output 1851 to 1884

Year	D'n & S't Ore (ozs)	U.K. Ore (ozs)	% of UK Ore Prod	Year	D'n & S't Ore (ozs)	U.K. Ore (ozs)	% of UK Ore Prod
1851	41,040	674,458	6.08	1868	39,865	841,328	4.74
1852	91,340	818,324	11.16	1869	27,437	831,891	3.30
1853	106,236	496,475	21.40	1870	24,706	784,562	3.15
1854	119,288	562,659	21.20	1871	13,805	761,490	1.81
1855	89,908	561,906	16.00	1872	10,392	628,920	1.65
1856	77,456	614,188	12.61	1873	6,510	524,307	1.24
1857	50,262	532,866	9.43	1874	8,209	509,277	1.61
1858	53,366	569,345	9.37	1875	4,542	487,358	0.93
1859	66,875	576,027	11.61	1876	5,890	483,422	1.22
1860	53,059	549,720	9.65	1877	6,503	497,375	1.31
1861	46,037	569,530	8.08	1878	4,836	397,471	1.22
1862	40,290	686,123	5.87	1879	1,915	333,674	0.57
1863	21,357	634,004	3.37	1880	226	295,518	0.08
1864	24,140	641,008	3.77	1881	60	308,398	0.02
1865	35,165	724,856	4.85	1882	65	372,449	0.02
1866	14,505	636,688	2.28	1883	2,400	344,053	0.70
1867	15,419	805,394	1.91	1884	2,760	325,718	0.85

Total 1,105,864 19,380,782 5.71

Table 4: Devon and Somerset Barytes ore production and its
share of total U.K. output 1877 to 1913

Year	D'n & S't Ore(tons)	U.K. Ore(tons)	% of UK Ore Prod	Year	D'n & S't Ore(tons)	U.K. Ore(tons)	% of UK Ore Prod
1877	1,843	21,057	8.75	1896	750	23,737	3.16
1878	313	22,437	1.40	1897	1,000	22,723	4.40
1879	-	19,349	0.00	1898	1,050	22,225	4.72
1880	30	17,476	0.17	1899	1,000	24,664	4.05
1881	615	21,313	2.89	1900	2,000	29,456	6.79
1882	510	23,308	2.19	1901	1,200	27,613	4.35
1883	656	21,396	3.07	1902	700	23,608	2.97
1884	593	20,062	2.96	1903	600	24,271	2.47
1885	-	26,153	0.00	1904	700	26,327	2.66
1886	800	25,142	3.18	1905	650	29,063	2.24
1887	1,000	24,831	4.03	1906	600	35,745	1.68
1888	-	25,191	0.00	1907	1,300	41,974	3.10
1889	1,200	24,849	4.83	1908	1,600	38,947	4.11
1890	2,000	25,353	7.89	1909	1,625	41,766	3.89
1891	2,600	26,876	9.67	1910	1,650	44,667	3.69
1892	2,705	24,247	11.16	1911	1,500	44,118	3.40
1893	1,659	22,343	7.43	1912	1,720	45,377	3.79
1894	900	20,656	4.36	1913	1,590	50,045	3.18
1895	500	21,170	2.36				

Total 39,159 1,029,535 3.80

Derbyshire mines included in production for 1892 and 1893.

Table 5

Devon and Somerset Fluorspar ore production and its share of total U.K. output 1856 to 1886

Year	D'n & S't Ore(tons)	U.K. Ore(tons)	% of UK Ore Prod	Year	D'n & S't Ore(tons)	U.K. Ore(tons)	% of UK Ore Prod
1856	1,017	1,490	68.26	1879	247	1,264	19.54
1857	1,025	1,173	87.38	1880	344	458	75.11
1858	738	790	93.42	1881	250	373	67.02
1874	609	632	96.36	1882	124	145	85.52
1875	324	359	90.25	1883	—	90	0.00
1876	338	338	100.00	1884	—	581	0.00
1877	—	—	0.00	1885	49	423	11.58
1878	7	391	1.79	1886	40	279	14.34
				Total	5,112	8,786	58.18

Returns of fluorspar production before the twentieth century probably seriously under-recorded output. This problem seems to have been resolved after 1901 but Devon and Somerset were nolonger producers.

Table 6

Devon and Somerset Zinc ore production and its share of total U.K. output 1856 to 1873

Year	D'n & S't Ore(tons)	U.K. Ore(tons)	% of UK Ore Prod	Year	D'n & S't Ore(tons)	U.K. Ore(tons)	% of UK Ore Prod
1856	660	9,004	7.34	1865	35	17,843	0.20
1857	775	9,290	8.35	1866	135	12,770	1.06
1858	392	11,556	3.40	1867	97	13,489	0.72
1859	288	13,039	2.22	1868	69	12,782	0.54
1860	217	15,553	1.40	1869	87	15,533	0.56
1861	50	15,770	0.32	1870	346	13,586	2.55
1862	25	7,498	0.34	1871	570	17,736	3.22
1863	73	13,699	0.53	1872	266	18,543	1.44
1864	59	15,232	0.39	1873	123	15,969	0.77
				Total	4,273	248,892	1.72

All zinc production came from Devon mines.

Table   7

Devon and Somerset Copper ore production and its share
of total U.K. output 1845 to 1913

Year	D'n & S't Ore(tons)	U.K. Ore(tons)	% of UK Ore Prod	Year	D'n & S't Ore(tons)	U.K. Ore(tons)	% of UK Ore Prod
1845	12,723	184,740	6.89	1880	15,760	52,128	30.23
1846	17,987	169,568	10.61	1881	17,133	52,556	32.60
1847	18,320	171,104	10.71	1882	19,201	52,237	36.76
1848	20,475	147,701	13.86	1883	18,197	46,820	38.87
1849	19,676	155,025	12.69	1884	18,081	42,149	42.90
1850	21,005	150,380	13.97	1885	15,002	36,379	41.24
1851	23,095	165,593	13.95	1886	10,076	18,617	54.12
1852	26,421	181,944	14.52	1887	5,184	9,359	55.39
1853	30,437	186,007	16.36	1888	6,936	15,550	44.60
1854	31,561	186,008	16.97	1889	2,659	9,310	28.56
1855	33,617	207,770	16.18	1890	6,038	12,481	48.38
1856	42,219	260,669	16.20	1891	4,039	9,158	44.10
1857	39,069	218,689	17.87	1892	2,823	6,265	45.06
1858	35,061	226,852	15.46	1893	2,471	5,576	44.31
1859	35,755	236,789	15.10	1894	2,314	5,994	38.61
1860	35,524	236,696	15.01	1895	2,008	7,791	25.77
1861	37,659	231,487	16.27	1896	1,588	9,168	17.32
1862	41,513	224,171	18.52	1897	1,417	7,352	19.27
1863	40,742	210,947	19.31	1898	1,084	9,131	11.87
1864	37,978	214,604	17.70	1899	990	8,319	11.90
1865	38,156	198,298	19.24	1900	1,016	9,488	10.71
1866	34,471	180,378	19.11	1901	848	6,792	12.49
1867	31,311	158,544	19.75	1902	350	6,112	5.73
1868	30,540	157,335	19.41	1903	-	6,867	0.00
1869	22,723	129,953	17.49	1904	210	5,465	3.84
1870	24,752	106,698	23.20	1905	834	7,153	11.66
1871	24,352	97,129	25.07	1906	1,117	7,758	14.40
1872	23,630	91,893	25.71	1907	685	6,792	10.09
1873	14,810	80,189	18.47	1908	681	5,441	12.52
1874	12,826	78,521	16.33	1909	461	3,717	12.40
1875	14,097	71,528	19.71	1910	18	4,178	0.43
1876	16,276	79,252	20.54	1911	18	3,262	0.55
1877	16,980	73,141	23.22	1912	21	1,933	1.09
1878	12,648	56,094	22.55	1913	27	2,732	0.99
1879	12,736	51,032	24.96				
				Total	1,090,432	6,070,759	17.96

Table 8

Devon and Somerset Arsenic and Arsenical Pyrites production
and its share of total U.K. output 1854 to 1913

Year	Arsenic D'n & S't Ore(tons)	Arsenic U.K. Ore(tons)	Arsenical Pyrites D'n & S't Ore(tons)	Arsenical Pyrites U.K. Ore(tons)	% of U.K. Prod. Arsenic	% of U.K. Prod. Arsenical Pyrites
1854	–	477	–	–	–	–
1855	344	787	344	495	43.70	69.50
1856	–	–	–	–	–	–
1857	–	477	–	–	–	–
1858	–	396	160	320	–	50.00
1859	20	465	–	–	4.30	–
1860	30	545	–	–	5.50	–
1861	672	1,211	–	–	55.50	–
1862	–	901	–	–	–	–
1863	–	721	–	–	–	–
1864	–	633	–	–	–	–
1865	–	827	–	–	–	–
1866	–	1,117	–	–	–	–
1867	56	1,256	–	–	4.50	–
1868	474	1,741	–	–	27.20	–
1869	1,373	2,562	2,444	2,444	53.60	100.00
1870	2,237	4,050	1,497	1,497	55.20	100.00
1871	2,220	6,368	1,731	1,731	34.90	100.00
1872	2,222	5,172	195	195	43.00	100.00
1873	1,969	5,449	–	–	36.10	–
1874	2,482	4,768	977	1,936	52.10	51.50
1875	2,157	4,569	801	7,489	47.20	10.70
1876	1,671	4,228	5,318	8,011	39.50	66.40
1877	3,092	4,810	1,050	14,929	64.30	7.00
1878	3,148	4,991	890	3,844	63.10	23.20
1879	3,833	5,492	1,948	2,843	69.80	68.50
1880	3,695	5,739	1,073	5,920	64.40	18.10
1881	3,381	6,156	1,397	14,338	54.90	9.70
1882	3,996	7,469	1,985	12,564	53.50	15.80
1883	4,242	7,622	535	1,300	55.70	41.20
1884	4,559	7,906	836	1,762	57.70	47.50
1885	4,240	8,129	1,766	1,911	52.20	92.40
1886	3,236	5,027	2,504	4,919	64.40	50.90
1887	2,957	4,618	4,262	4,363	64.00	97.70
1888	3,040	4,624	3,882	5,325	65.70	72.90
1889	2,831	4,758	5,245	7,688	59.50	68.20
1890	4,133	7,276	3,578	5,114	56.80	70.00
1891	3,001	6,049	3,991	5,095	49.60	78.30

Table 8(cont)

Year	Arsenic D'n & S't Ore(tons)	Arsenic U.K. Ore(tons)	Arsenical Pyrites D'n & S't Ore(tons)	Arsenical Pyrites U.K. Ore(tons)	% of U.K. Prod. Arsenic	% of U.K. Prod. Arsenical Pyrites
1892	2,547	5,114	3,411	6,497	49.80	75.90
1893	4,225	5,976	2,201	3,036	70.70	72.50
1894	2,901	4,801	1,769	3,288	60.40	53.80
1895	2,977	4,798	1,374	2,931	62.10	46.90
1896	2,250	3,616	2,604	8,808	62.20	29.60
1897	3,151	4,165	1,623	13,137	75.70	12.40
1898	3,112	4,174	1,415	12,559	74.60	11.30
1899	2,468	3,829	3,750	13,429	64.50	27.90
1900	2,921	4,081	554	9,573	71.60	5.80
1901	2,103	3,361	244	2,578	62.60	9.50
1902	1,102	2,131	294	829	51.70	35.50
1903	212	902	57	57	23.50	100.00
1904	149	976	–	43	15.30	–
1905	5	1,528	594	641	0.30	92.70
1906	–	1,599	307	640	–	48.00
1907	129	1,497	482	689	8.60	70.00
1908	510	1,919	1,925	1,925	26.60	100.00
1909	1,048	2,865	93	93	36.60	100.00
1910	336	2,153	61	684	15.60	8.90
1911	205	2,121	20	1,170	9.70	1.70
1912	255	2,266	–	1,778	11.30	–
1913	203	1,652	–	35	12.30	–
Total	104,120	204,910	71,207	198,454	50.80	35.90

All U.K. arsenic production came from mines in Cornwall and Devon, except for 4 tons produced from Carrock Fell in Cumberland in 1911.

Table 9

Devon and Somerset Manganese ore production and its share
of total U.K. output 1858 to 1913

Year	D'N & S't Ore(tons)	U.K. Ore(tons)	% of UK Ore Prod	Year	D'N & S't Ore(tons)	U.K. Ore(tons)	% of UK Ore Prod
1858	1,400	1,400	100.00	1886	1,015	12,763	7.95
1859	1,231	1,231	100.00	1887	335	13,777	2.43
1860	932	932	100.00	1888	156	4,342	3.59
1861	926	926	100.00	1889	—	8,852	0.00
1862	—	—	0.00	1890	223	12,444	1.79
1863	—	—	0.00	1891	180	9,476	1.90
1864	—	—	0.00	1892	840	6,078	13.82
1865	—	—	0.00	1893	325	1,336	24.33
1866	—	—	0.00	1894	31	1,809	1.71
1867	796	808	98.51	1895	389	1,273	30.56
1868	1,700	1,750	97.14	1896	—	1,080	0.00
1869	1,558	1,558	100.00	1897	—	599	0.00
1870	4,839	4,839	100.00	1898	—	231	0.00
1871	5,548	5,548	100.00	1899	—	415	0.00
1872	7,723	7,773	99.36	1900	—	1,362	0.00
1873	8,654	8,671	99.80	1901	—	1,646	0.00
1874	5,643	5,778	97.66	1902	120	1,278	9.39
1875	3,165	3,206	98.72	1903	15	818	1.83
1876	2,645	2,797	94.57	1904	177	8,756	2.02
1877	2,459	3,039	80.91	1905	122	14,474	0.84
1878	1,200	1,586	75.66	1906	24	22,762	0.11
1879	497	816	60.91	1907	34	16,098	0.21
1880	1,560	2,839	54.95	1908	—	6,308	0.00
1881	1,405	2,884	48.72	1909	—	2,768	0.00
1882	957	1,548	61.82	1910	—	5,467	0.00
1883	1,108	1,287	86.09	1911	—	4,987	0.00
1884	646	909	71.07	1912	—	4,170	0.00
1885	1,498	1,688	88.74	1913	—	5,393	0.00
				Total	62,076	234,575	26.46

The Devon and Somerset total for 1867–8 includes some production from
Cornwall. For all other years the output was only from Devon mines, with
the exception of 1881–2, 1884, 1890–1 and 1895 when there was a small
output from Somerset.

Table 10

Devon and Somerset Iron ore production and its share
of total U.K. output 1855 to 1913

Year	D'n & S't Ore(tons)	U.K. Ore(tons)	% of UK Ore Prod	Year	D'n & S't Ore(tons)	U.K. Ore(tons)	% of UK Ore Prod
1855	6,440	9,553,741	0.07	1885	4,027	15,417,982	0.03
1856	18,720	10,483,309	0.18	1886	5,041	14,110,013	0.04
1857	27,842	9,372,781	0.30	1887	4,105	13,098,041	0.03
1858	30,795	8,040,959	0.38	1888	3,473	14,590,713	0.02
1859	32,682	7,876,582	0.41	1889	4,630	14,546,105	0.03
1860	27,938	8,035,306	0.35	1890	4,791	13,780,767	0.03
1861	38,162	7,215,518	0.53	1891	5,076	12,777,689	0.04
1862	34,963	7,562,240	0.46	1892	3,437	11,312,675	0.03
1863	41,723	8,613,951	0.48	1893	933	11,203,476	0.01
1864	63,993	10,064,891	0.64	1894	230	12,367,308	0.00
1865	75,798	9,910,046	0.76	1895	2,343	12,615,414	0.02
1866	75,994	9,665,013	0.79	1896	12,418	13,700,764	0.09
1867	47,087	10,021,058	0.47	1897	1,694	13,787,878	0.01
1868	43,628	10,169,231	0.43	1898	4,974	14,176,936	0.04
1869	34,334	11,508,526	0.30	1899	3,429	14,461,330	0.02
1870	29,933	14,496,427	0.21	1900	6,493	14,028,208	0.05
1871	47,009	16,470,010	0.29	1901	636	12,275,198	0.01
1872	60,274	15,755,675	0.38	1902	1,362	13,426,004	0.01
1873	56,046	15,583,669	0.36	1903	193	13,715,645	0.00
1874	62,655	14,844,936	0.42	1904	322	13,774,282	0.00
1875	55,760	15,821,060	0.35	1905	415	14,590,703	0.00
1876	54,235	16,841,584	0.32	1906	461	15,500,406	0.00
1877	58,362	16,692,802	0.35	1907	432	15,731,604	0.00
1878	47,608	15,726,370	0.30	1908	4,277	15,031,025	0.03
1879	14,693	14,379,735	0.10	1909	2,053	14,979,979	0.01
1880	41,971	18,026,050	0.23	1910	3,683	15,226,015	0.02
1881	41,081	17,446,065	0.24	1911	732	15,519,424	0.00
1882	47,548	18,031,957	0.26	1912	981	13,790,391	0.01
1883	19,635	17,383,046	0.11	1913	1,390	15,997,328	0.01
1884	4,885	16,137,887	0.03				
				Total	1,325,825	787,263,728	0.17

Tables of Mine Production,

Ownership, Management and

Employment

Section A

The Devonshire

Returns

```
ADAMS                        CHRISTOW                        SX 836837 0001

Production: Lead & Silver    Ore(tons)  Lead(tons) Silver(ozs)    Value(£)
            1845                59.00      29.00
            1846                33.00      16.00
            1847               250.00     150.00
            1848                56.00      30.00
            1849               382.00     210.00
            1850               395.00     217.10
            1851               230.00     126.30
            1852        /       70.00      38.50      680.00
            1854-1857 No detailed return
            Comment 1854-1857 SEE EXMOUTH
            Zinc             Ore(tons) Metal(tons)       Value(£)
            1859        No detailed return
            Comment 1859 SEE ADDAMS, CORNWALL
            Copper No detailed return
Ownership:  Comment 1860-1865 SEE NORTH EXMOUTH
Management: Manager 1859 HY.HARVEY
            Secretary 1859 G.LAVINGTON (P)


ALBION                       ILSINGTON                       SX 778762 0002

Production: Tin No detailed return
Ownership:  1913 ALBION TIN SYNDICATE
            Comment 1913 REOPENING NOV.1913
Management: Manager 1913 W.H.HOSKING
Employment:               Underground    Surface      Total
            1913              4             4            8


ALLER                        CHRISTOW                        SX 834840 0003

Production: Lead & Silver No detailed return
Ownership:  1876-1879 ALLER SILVER LEAD MINING CO.
Management: Chief Agent 1877-1879 J.D.HARRIS
            Secretary 1877-1879 T.WATSON DUNCAN (S)
Employment:               Underground    Surface      Total
            1878             12             9           21


ALLIFORD                     MARYSTOWE                       SX 423853 0004

Production: Manganese        Ore(tons) Metal(tons)       Value(£)
            1868        No detailed return
            1872             42.00                        210.00
            Comment 1868 SEE CHILLATON
Management: Manager 1868-1872 C.JOHN SIMS & F.SIMS; 1873 WM.DOIDGE
            Secretary 1868-1872 C.JOHN SIMS & F.SIMS; 1873 SIMS BROS
```

1

AMERY   CHRISTOW   SX 835839 0005

Production: Lead & Silver No detailed return
Ownership: Comment 1860-1865 SEE NORTH EXMOUTH
Management: Manager 1859 HY.HARVEY
            Secretary 1859 G.LAVINGTON (P)

ANDERTON   WHITCHURCH   SX 485723 0006

Production: Tin   Black(tons) Stuff(tons) Tin(tons)   Value(£)
            1882   37.30   23.00   2002.00
            1883   43.40   2385.00
            1884   7.00   286.00
            1885   13.90   541.00
            1886   32.70   1749.00
            1887   38.60   2459.00
            1888   24.90   1539.00
            1889   4.00   150.00   190.00
            Comment 1888-1889 ANDERTON UNITED
Ownership: 1882-1889 ANDERTON TIN MINING CO.
            Comment 1889 NOW ABANDONED
Management: Chief Agent 1882-1884 W.J.BOWHAY; 1885-1889 JOHN GOLDSWORTHY
Employment: Underground   Surface   Total
            1882   8   8   16
            1883   17   21   38
            1884   12   11   23
            1885   11   11   22
            1886   36   20   56
            1887   39   25   64
            1888   26   20   46
            1889   16   12   28

ANNA MARIA   TAVISTOCK   0007

Production: Copper No detailed return

ARCHER   DODDISCOMBSLEIGH   SX 858862 0008

Production: Manganese No detailed return
Management: Manager 1874-1875 JAS.RODDA

ARTHUR   CALSTOCK, CORNWALL   SX 432700 0009

Production: Copper   Ore(tons) Metal(tons)   Value(£)
            1857   1132.00   43.00   3843.10
            1858   481.00   17.80   1445.10
            Comment 1857-1858 (C)
            Tin   Black(tons) Stuff(tons) Tin(tons)   Value(£)
            1855   6.00   406.60
Ownership: 1880 WHEAL ARTHUR MINING CO.; 1894 MOSES BOWDEN & CO.
Management: Chief Agent 1880 MOSES BOWDEN

2

Employment: Underground   Surface   Total
            1894   1   1

ARUNDEL MINES   BUCKFASTLEIGH   SX 744716 0010

Ownership: Comment 1866-1870 SEE DRUID

ASHBURTON UNITED   ASHBURTON   SX 771733 0012

Production: Copper No detailed return
            Tin   Black(tons) Stuff(tons) Tin(tons)   Value(£)
            1860   111.40   8761.60
            1861   84.20   6256.00
            1862   93.00   6396.70
            Arsenic   Ore(tons) Metal(tons)   Value(£)
            1859   20.00   38.00
            1860   29.80   55.80
            Comment 1859-1860 CRUDE ARSENIC
Ownership: Comment 1862-1866 OR WEST BEAM
Management: Manager 1859-1863 WM.EDWARDS; 1864-1866 W.H.HOSKING
            Chief Agent 1861-1863 E.HARVEY
            Secretary 1860-1866 THOS.GILLFORD (P)

ASHBURTON,EAST   ILSINGTON   0013

Production: Copper No detailed return
            Tin No detailed return
Management: Manager 1872 JAS.RICHARDS
            Chief Agent 1875 JAS.RICHARDS
            Secretary 1875 BETTELEY,HORSWILL & CO.

ASHBURTON,WEST   ASHBURTON   0014

Production: Copper No detailed return
            Tin No detailed return
Ownership: Comment 1863-1865 SUSPENDED
Management: Chief Agent 1860-1862 WM.RICHARDS
            Secretary 1860-1862 ROBT.JORY (P)

ATLAS   ILSINGTON   SX 778762 0015

Production: Tin   Black(tons) Stuff(tons) Tin(tons)   Value(£)
            1862   4.00   238.80
            1863   3.80   233.50
            1890   19.10   1119.00
            1891   14.30   804.00
            1892   6.20   305.00
            1893   3.60   183.00

Tin	Black(tons)	Stuff(tons)	Tin(tons)	Value(£)
1901	0.70			54.00
1902	1.00			76.00
1903	4.60			354.00

Comment 1862 PART YEAR ONLY
Ownership: 1889-1890 ATLAS TIN MINING CO.; 1891-1898 ATLAS TIN MINING
             CO.LTD.; 1899 DANIEL & THOMAS; 1900-1902 ATLAS TIN MINING
             CO.; 1903-1908 ATLAS TIN MINING CO.LTD.
             Comment 1864-1865 SUSPENDED; 1894 NOT WORKED IN 1894;
             1895-1898 IN LIQUIDATION; 1905-1908 SUSPENDED
Management: Chief Agent 1860-1863 J.WARREN; 1889-1898 WM.GROSE
             Secretary 1861-1863 JOS.HARRIS; 1891-1894 F.W.THOMAS (S)

Employment:	Underground	Surface	Total
1889	18	19	37
1890	27	18	45
1891	15	6	21
1892	6	5	11
1893	5	4	9
1895	4		4
1900	4	2	6
1901	7	4	11
1902	9	4	13
1903	4	4	8

ATLAS IRON   ILSINGTON   SX 778762 0016

Production: Iron	Ore(tons)	Iron(%)	Value(£)
1864	1300.00		637.50

Comment 1864 BH.
Ownership: 1863 ATLAS MINING CO.; 1864-1865 WM.BROWNE
             Comment 1864-1865 INC. SMALLACOMBE; 1866 SEE SMALLACOMBE
Management: Chief Agent 1863 J.DUNN; 1865 WM.GROSE

ATWAY   LAUNCESTON, CORNWALL   SX 305861 0017

Production: Manganese No detailed return
Ownership: Comment 1880-1881 SEE EAST CHILLATON

BAGTOR   ILSINGTON   SX 762759 0018

Production: Copper No detailed return

Tin	Black(tons)	Stuff(tons)	Tin(tons)	Value(£)
1863	4.20			275.40
1864	3.50			209.80
1865	7.00			401.50

Production: Copper

	Ore(tons)	Metal(tons)	Value(£)
1856	49.00	6.70	664.50
1857	195.00	31.80	3409.10
1858	210.00	30.80	3078.90
1859	199.00	24.10	2378.00
1860	233.00	29.20	2826.50
1861	51.00	8.70	849.10
1862	237.00	45.10	3914.80
1863	390.00	62.10	5125.70
1864	376.00	53.30	4871.70
1865	449.00	67.20	5496.70
1866	493.00	71.90	5278.70
1867	459.00	71.80	5223.60
1868	294.00	44.50	3133.90
1869	451.00	67.20	4629.10
1870	235.00	34.70	2236.70
1871	20.00	3.60	245.50
1872	198.00	18.40	1378.20
1873	62.00	7.40	550.50
1874	312.00	27.50	1960.00
1875	304.00	28.50	2190.20
1876	39.00	3.90	292.50
1878	62.00	5.90	397.60
1879	8.80	0.90	49.20
1880	7.00	0.80	35.00

Comment 1856-1857 (S) BAMFYLDE; 1858-1859 (S); 1860 (C)(S);
1861 (S); 1862 (C)(S); 1863-1871 (C); 1872 (C)(S); 1873-1876
(S) BAMFYLDE; 1878-1879 (I)(S); 1880 (I)

Manganese

	Ore(tons)	Metal(tons)	Value(£)
1873	50.00		337.50
1874	No detailed return		
1875	36.00		180.00

Comment 1873-1875 BAMFYLDE
Tin No detailed return

Iron

	Ore(tons)	Iron(%)	Value(£)
1873	1800.00		1350.00
1874	417.80		206.50
1875	22.00		11.00
1879	5.20		2.60
1880	1309.20		785.40
1881	1879.30		1127.40
1882	1684.00		505.00

1883-1885 No detailed return
Comment 1873-1875 SP.; 1879-1880 SP.; 1881-1882 BH.

Ownership: 1873-1875 BAMPFYLDE COPPER MINING CO.; 1876-1882 BAMPFYLDE
MINING CO.LTD.; 1883-1884 NORTH MOLTON MINING CO.; 1885-1886
NORTH DEVON MINING CO.LTD.
Comment 1860-1862 BAMFYLDE; 1869-1872 NEW BAMPFYLDE;
1880-1882 IN LIQUIDATION; 1883 NOT WORKED IN 1883; 1884 NOT
WORKED IN 1884; 1885 NOT WORKED IN 1885; 1886 NOT WORKED IN
1886; 1887 SEE STOWFORD

Management: Manager 1873 SML.MITCHELL; 1874-1881 J.JULEFF
Chief Agent 1860-1872 JOS.POPE; 1874-1877 H.T.HALEY;

BAMPFYLDE NORTH MOLTON Continued

1883-1886 G.KEY KLINGENDER
Secretary 1861-1872 CHAS.HAND (P); 1873-1882 G.KEY KLINGENDER

Employment:

	Underground	Surface	Total
1878	12	7	19
1879		11	11
1880	2	11	13
1881	8	5	13
1882	6	5	11
1887			

Comment 1887 SEE STOWFORD

BARTON TORQUAY 0020

Production: Iron No detailed return
Ownership: 1873 WM.BROWNE
Management: Manager 1873 PHAR.GROSE

BEAM SX 767734 0021

Production: Tin

	Black(tons)	Stuff(tons)	Tin(tons)	Value(£)
1854	2.00			139.60

BEAM,WEST ASHBURTON SX 771733 0022

Production: Copper No detailed return
Tin

	Black(tons)	Stuff(tons)	Tin(tons)	Value(£)
1853	1.70			118.20
1862	31.50			2201.50
1863	57.80			4042.50
1864	34.80			2285.30
1865	29.90			1745.10
1866	30.40			1662.70

Comment 1853 DEVON WEST BEAM; 1862 PART YEAR ONLY; 1865 WEST BEAM MINING CO.
Ownership: Comment 1862-1866 SEE ASHBURTON UNITED; 1881 SEE OWLACOMBE

* BEDFORD TAVISTOCK SX 473700 0023 *

Production: Copper

	Ore(tons)	Metal(tons)	Value(£)
1852	267.00	10.60	742.70

Comment 1852 (C)

* BEDFORD CONSOLS TAVISTOCK 0024 *

Production: Copper

	Ore(tons)	Metal(tons)	Value(£)
1862	21.00	0.80	52.00
1869	9.00	0.50	30.10

BEDFORD CONSOLS   TAVISTOCK   Continued

          Copper   Ore(tons) Metal(tons)   Value(£)
          1875   17.00   1.00   85.00
          Comment 1862 (C); 1869 (C); 1875 (C)
          Tin No detailed return
          Arsenic Pyrite Ore(tons)   Value(£)
          1875   211.30   318.50
          1876   85.00   122.80
          1877   30.50   38.00
          Comment 1876 VALUE INCL STENS INN PYNTEC; 1877 ARSENICAL
          MUNDIC
Management: Manager 1859-1875 JOS.MITCHELL; 1876 GEO.ROWE
          Chief Agent 1859 JOS.MITCHELL; 1876 GEO.ROWE JUN.
          Secretary 1859-1863 JOS.MATTHEWS (P); 1864-1868 WM.ROWSE;
          1869-1870 THOS.HORSWILL; 1871-1876 GEO.ROWE

✳ BEDFORD UNITED   TAVISTOCK   SX 441726 0025 ✳

Production: Copper   Ore(tons) Metal(tons)   Value(£)
          1845   1297.00   125.20   8744.10
          1846   1158.00   108.90   6960.90
          1847   1355.00   148.40   10239.70
          1848   1314.00   129.60   7471.40
          1849   1415.00   148.60   10150.80
          1850   1426.00   138.70   9804.10
          1851   1700.00   154.80   10341.70
          1852   1871.00   141.90   11986.00
          1853   1926.00   139.40   13990.60
          1854   2136.00   156.50   15441.80
          1855   2292.00   155.20   15750.40
          1856   2391.00   148.30   13607.30
          1857   2542.00   155.50   15120.30
          1858   2529.00   150.50   13308.10
          1859   2503.00   157.30   14576.30
          1860   2452.00   153.40   13342.30
          1861   2449.00   145.10   12476.20
          1862   2545.00   148.30   11650.60
          1863   2444.00   139.70   10391.50
          1864   2357.00   132.70   11383.80
          1865   1909.00   100.30   8137.20
          1866   1418.00   87.10   5976.80
          1867   1214.00   61.70   4399.50
          1868   1104.00   50.10   3204.00
          1869   985.00   48.20   2933.80
          1870   946.00   48.60   2845.10
          1871   867.00   45.90   2843.10
          1872   1090.00   49.50   3568.90
          1873   780.00   37.90   2205.80
          1874   948.00   53.50   3441.50
          1875   1018.00   61.20   4701.10
          1876   643.00   34.60   2350.80
          1877   932.60   59.00   3195.50
          1878   1151.00   69.60   3322.60

                              7

Copper	Ore(tons)	Metal(tons)	Value(£)
1879	674.80	50.80	2559.20
1880	653.90	44.60	2315.90
1881	656.00	38.10	1997.40
1882	950.70	67.50	3922.00
1883	1569.00	109.80	5634.00
1884	2311.00		6964.00
1885	1455.00		3872.00
1886	683.00		2250.00
1887	258.00		589.00
1888	118.00		694.00
1889	20.00		65.00

Comment 1845-1874 (C); 1875-1876 (C) BEDFORD

Tin	Black(tons)	Stuff(tons)	Tin(tons)	Value(£)
1906	6.90			730.00
1909	8.50			595.00
1910	2.70			250.00
1911	0.70			70.00
1912	0.80			115.00
1913	4.00			502.00

Comment 1906 BEDFORD,VALUE EST.; 1909-1913 BEDFORD,VALUE
EST.

Arsenic	Ore(tons)	Metal(tons)	Value(£)
1855	197.00		

Comment 1855 ARSENICAL MUNDIC

Fluorspar	Ore(tons)	Value(£)
1875	44.30	25.10
1878	7.40	7.00
1879	7.00	7.00

Tungsten	Ore(tons)	Metal(tons)	Value(£)
1900	1.00		39.00
1903	3.00		45.00
1906	11.60		896.00
1909	10.20		
1910	4.70		
1911	1.30		
1912	0.40		
1913	2.50		

Comment 1906 BEDFORD, VALUE EST.; 1909-1913 BEDFORD

Arsenic Pyrite	Ore(tons)	Value(£)
1869	261.30	163.30
1870	223.50	139.70
1871	198.50	124.10
1872	195.30	122.10
1874	28.00	21.00
1875	136.20	85.00
1876	222.00	220.60
1877	254.00	169.30
1878	443.00	295.30
1879	204.00	143.20
1880	144.00	114.40
1881	172.10	141.10
1882	935.10	799.00

8

Arsenic Pyrite	Ore(tons)	Value(£)
1883	451.00	444.00
1884	814.80	936.00
1885	1616.00	1308.00
1886	2004.00	1351.00
1887	1743.00	1291.00
1888	1037.00	879.00
1889	285.00	262.00
1897	36.00	51.00
1900	12.00	15.00
1903	57.00	57.00
1905	500.00	
1906	30.00	36.00
1907	363.00	318.00
1908	223.00	250.00
1909	93.00	150.00
1910	61.00	100.00
1911	20.00	30.00

Comment 1876-1877 ARSENICAL MUNDIC; 1905 VALUE NOT EST MIXED
ORE AR,WO,SN,& CU; 1906-1911 BEDFORD,VALUE EST.

Ownership: 1868-1876 THOS.HORSWILL (P); 1877-1878 BEDFORD UNITED MINING
CO.; 1879-1890 BEDFORD UNITED MINING CO.LTD.; 1897 WM.JACKMAN
& OTHERS; 1900-1903 WM.PHILLIPS; 1904-1910 F.BOEHM; 1911-1913
BRITISH MINING & METAL CO.LTD.
Comment 1889 IN LIQUIDATION; 1890 NOW ABANDONED; 1904-1913
BEDFORD

Management: Manager 1859-1863 JAS.WOLFERSTAN; 1864-1869 JAS.PHILLIPS;
1877-1881 THOS.HORSWILL
Chief Agent 1859 JAS.PHILLIPS; 1861-1863 JAS.PHILLIPS;
1864-1876 WM.PHILLIPS; 1877-1881 RICH.GOLDSWORTHY; 1882-1887
HY.TREZISE; 1888 THOS.HORSWILL; 1905-1912 J.H.HEAP
Secretary 1859 JAS.WOLFERSTAN (P); 1860 T.B.LAWS (P);
1861-1863 JAS.WOLFERSTAN (P); 1864-1867 THOS.HORSWILL (P);
1869-1881 T.B.LAWS (S); 1889 THOS.HORSWILL (P)

Employment:

	Underground	Surface	Total
1878	48	33	81
1879	41	23	64
1880	35	35	70
1881	39	28	67
1882	66	42	108
1883	68	41	109
1884	85	45	130
1885	64	49	113
1886	54	33	87
1887	35	31	66
1888	25	21	46
1889	7	9	16
1897	2		2
1900	2		2
1901	3		3
1902-1903	5		5
1904	23	7	30
1905	27	22	49

	Underground	Surface	Total
1906	30	27	57
1907	35	22	57
1909	12	21	33
1910	11	15	26
1911	3	19	22
1912	4	17	21
1913	6	9	15

 BEDFORD,SOUTH   TAVISTOCK   SX 435718 0026 ✳

Production: Copper

	Ore(tons)	Metal(tons)	Value(£)
1854	162.00	7.00	622.00
1855	380.00	17.30	1628.30
1856	619.00	26.10	2121.40
1857	466.00	16.40	1393.50
1858	308.00	10.50	813.00
1859	479.00	18.20	1450.30
1860	617.00	23.70	1848.70
1861	775.00	28.80	2182.50
1862	624.00	24.50	1743.90
1863	280.00	10.40	641.70
1864	209.00	8.40	620.50
1865	52.00	2.10	141.10
1873	No detailed return		

Comment 1854 (C) SOUTH BEDFORD CONSOLS; 1855 (C) SOUTH
BEDFORD CONSOLS & EAST GUNNISL; 1856 (C) EAST GUNNISLAKE &
SOUTH BEDFORD; 1857 (C); 1858 (C) SOUTH BEDFORD & EAST
GUNNISLAKE; 1859-1865 (C); 1870 (C) SEE EAST
GUNNISLAKE,CORNWALL; 1873 SEE EAST GUNNISLAKE,CORNWALL

Tin

	Black(tons)	Stuff(tons)	Tin(tons)	Value(£)
1860	No detailed return			
1862	No detailed return			

Comment 1860 SEE EAST GUNNISLAKE; 1862 SEE EAST GUNNISLAKE

Ownership: 1870-1871 J.H.DENNIS (P)
Comment 1859-1875 INC.EAST GUNNISLAKE

Management: Manager 1859-1866 W.G.GARD
Chief Agent 1859-1866 JOHN PHILLIPS; 1867-1869 JAS.BRAY;
1872-1875 JAS.BRAY
Secretary 1859-1866 W.G.GARD (P); 1867-1868 RICH.DENNIS; 1869
T.B.LAWS; 1870-1871 JAS.BRAY (S); 1872-1875 J.H.DENNIS (S)

✳ BELSTONE   BELSTONE   SX 632945 0027 ✳

Production: Copper

	Ore(tons)	Metal(tons)	Value(£)
1867	268.00	32.60	1875.40
1868	174.00	14.10	969.60
1869	201.00	19.80	1313.20
1870	57.00	5.90	373.30
1871	43.00	5.10	342.20
1872	105.00	11.80	929.00

Copper	Ore(tons)	Metal(tons)	Value(£)
1873	100.00	10.40	724.20
1874	54.00	4.80	338.70
1875	35.00	3.20	247.80
1876	116.00	11.10	798.00
1877	134.10	13.00	783.00
1878	No detailed return		
1880-1881	No detailed return		

Comment 1867 (C)(P); 1867 (C); 1868-1877 (C); 1878 SEE MID
DEVON; 1880-1881 SEE MID DEVON

Arsenic Pyrite	Ore(tons)	Value(£)
1875	13.70	17.20
1884	21.00	24.00

Ownership: 1877 BELSTON MINING CO.LTD.; 1878-1879 MID.DEVON COPPER
MINING CO.LTD.; 1884-1886 MID.DEVON COPPER MINING CO.
Comment 1878-1879 NOW MID.DEVON; 1880-1882 SEE MID.DEVON;
1887-1890 SEE MID.DEVON; 1905-1911 SEE RAMSLEY

Management: Manager 1868 J.YORK; 1869-1870 OLI.YORK; 1871-1879 JAS.NEILL
Chief Agent 1867 J.G.MARTIN; 1884-1886 JAS.NEILL
Secretary 1867-1868 S.W.WILKINSON; 1869-1876 F.R.REEVES

Employment:	Underground	Surface	Total
1884	10	8	18
1885	12	12	24
1886	18	13	31
1887-1890			

＊ BERTHA CONSOLS   BUCKLAND MONACHORUM   SX 471689 0028 ＊

Production: Copper	Ore(tons)	Metal(tons)	Value(£)
1888	227.00		1017.00
1889	409.00		767.00
1890	30.00		35.00
1891	90.00		112.00
1892	19.00		64.00
1893	114.00		2040.00
1894	67.00		84.00

Tin	Black(tons)	Stuff(tons)	Tin(tons)	Value(£)
1893	1.10			40.00
1895	2.10			80.00
1896	2.00			74.00

Comment 1893 BERTH CONSOLS; 1895-1896 BERTH CONSOLS

Arsenic	Ore(tons)	Metal(tons)	Value(£)
1890	964.00		1271.00
1894	216.00		2376.00
1895	201.00		2000.00
1896	112.00		1680.00
1897	131.00		2489.00
1898	70.00		980.00
1899	20.00		340.00

Arsenic Pyrite	Ore(tons)	Value(£)
1888	750.00	562.00
1889	1805.00	2120.00

11

Arsenic Pyrite	Ore(tons)	Value(£)
1891	810.00	911.00
1892	1475.00	1475.00
1893	333.00	114.00

Ownership: 1887-1899 BERTHA CONSOLS LTD.
Comment 1899 CLOSED JAN.1900
Management: Chief Agent 1887-1889 THOS.GREGORY; 1890 THOS.GREGORY &
WM.GILL; 1891 WM.GILL; 1898-1899 WM.B.SKEWIS
Secretary 1891-1895 WM.B.SKEWIS (S)

Employment:

	Underground	Surface	Total
1888	30	11	41
1889	30	8	38
1890	14	10	24
1891	22	10	32
1892	33	15	48
1893	49	12	61
1894	44	26	70
1895	37	37	74
1896	36	34	70
1897	42	37	79
1898	9	7	16

✳ BERTHA CONSOLS,EAST   BUCKLAND MONACHORUM   SX 478690 0029✳

Production: Copper No detailed return
Ownership: Comment 1862-1865 SUSPENDED
Management: Manager 1859 WM.GOSS; 1860-1861 JAS.RICHARDS
Chief Agent 1859 ?JENKINS; 1860-1861 S.COCK
Secretary 1859-1865 THOS.FULLER (P)

✳ BERTHA,EAST LADY   BUCKLAND MONACHORUM   SX 478690 0030✳

Production: Copper No detailed return
Management: Chief Agent 1866 W.E.CUMMINS

✳ BERTHA,LADY   BUCKLAND MONACHORUM   SX 471689 0031✳

Production: Copper

	Ore(tons)	Metal(tons)	Value(£)
1855	86.00	6.00	572.90
1856	479.00	25.80	2280.10
1857	210.00	9.60	965.70
1858	317.00	13.50	1100.20
1859	784.00	40.30	3546.30
1860	1103.00	58.10	4913.30
1861	1289.00	52.30	4070.70
1862	1311.00	52.50	3781.90
1863	620.00	24.40	1579.10
1864	337.00	11.60	826.70
1865	342.00	13.30	915.30
1866	336.00	12.50	718.00

Copper	Ore(tons)	Metal(tons)	Value(£)
1867	16.00	1.00	71.90
1881	42.00	2.50	126.00
1882	100.00	4.00	150.00

Comment 1855-1867 (C)

Arsenic Pyrite	Ore(tons)	Value(£)
1881	632.00	505.60
1882	1050.00	814.00

Ownership: 1880-1883 LADY BERTHA UNITED MINING CO.LTD.
Comment 1883 NOT WORKED IN 1883
Management: Manager 1859-1866 F.C.HARPER; 1880-1881 THOS.NEILL
Chief Agent 1859-1866 J.METHERELL; 1875-1876 RICH.HAWKE;
1882-1883 THOS.GREGORY
Secretary 1859-1866 W.E.CUMMINS (P); 1875-1876 H.N.LAY

Employment:	Underground	Surface	Total
1880	9	9	18
1881	40	5	45
1882	20	5	25

BERTHA,NEW EAST   BUCKLAND MONACHORUM   0032

Production: Copper No detailed return
Ownership: Comment 1862-1865 SUSPENDED
Management: Chief Agent 1860-1861 S.COCK

BERTHA,SOUTH LADY   BUCKLAND MONACHORUM   SX 477682 0033

Production: Copper No detailed return
Ownership: Comment 1862-1865 SUSPENDED
Management: Manager 1860-1861 JOS.RICHARDS
Chief Agent 1859 JOS.RICHARDS & RICH.UNSWORTH; 1860-1861
RICH.UNSWORTH
Secretary 1859-1865 JOS.RICHARDS (P)

BETSY   MARYTAVY   SX 510812 0034

Production: Lead & Silver	Ore(tons)	Lead(tons)	Silver(ozs)	Value(£)
1845	296.00	148.00		
1846	58.50	29.00		
1847	7.00	3.50		
1848	6.00	3.00		
1858	19.00	12.20	245.00	
1869	20.30	15.30		
1870	168.90	126.00	500.00	
1871	106.50	74.20	297.00	
1872	71.60	49.70	198.00	
1873	77.50	53.90	215.00	1051.30
1874	70.70	49.60	198.00	781.80
1875	35.50	25.50	116.00	
1876	57.10	42.50	250.00	702.50

Lead & Silver	Ore(tons)	Lead(tons)	Silver(ozs)	Value(£)
1877	1.60	0.80		22.00

Zinc No detailed return

Ownership: 1872-1873 R.DONALDSON & CO.; 1876 WHEAL BETSY CO.; 1877
JAS.WATSON & CO.
Comment 1863-1870 SEE PRINCE ARTHUR CONSOLS; 1871 BELSY SEE
PRINCE ARTHUR CONSOLS; 1872 BELSY
Management: Manager 1872 WM.GEORGE; 1873-1874 ROBT.JORY; 1875-1877
WM.GEORGE
Chief Agent 1874 WM.GEORGE
Secretary 1872-1873 WM.GEORGE; 1874-1875 R.DONALDSON; 1876
WM.GEORGE

⚹ BETSY,SOUTH   MARYTAVY   SX 511809 0035 ⚹

Production: Lead & Silver	Ore(tons)	Lead(tons)	Silver(ozs)	Value(£)
1859	22.00	12.00	348.00	
1860	18.50	14.00	119.00	

1861   No detailed return
Copper No detailed return
Ownership: Comment 1862-1865 SUSPENDED
Management: Manager 1859-1861 THOS.NEILL
Chief Agent 1859-1861 WM.STEPHENS
Secretary 1859-1865 GEO.DOWN (P)

⚹ BICKLEY VALE PHOENIX   BICKLEIGH   SX 531642 0036 ⚹

Production: Lead No detailed return
Ownership: Comment 1862-1865 SUSPENDED
Management: Chief Agent 1860 J.PHILLIPS & F.HAMBLY; 1861 JOHN HAMBLY
Secretary 1860-1865 H.BENNETT (P)

Part in ?

BIRCH ALLER   BRIDFORD   SX 828869 0037

Production: Lead & Silver	Ore(tons)	Lead(tons)	Silver(ozs)	Value(£)
1854	13.50	9.00	126.00	
1855	12.00	7.00		

BIRCH TOR AND VITIFER   NORTH BOVEY   SX 680810 0038

Production: Tin	Black(tons)	Stuff(tons)	Tin(tons)	Value(£)
1852	15.20			
1853	16.50			1194.50
1854	22.20			1443.10
1855	8.50			513.00
1856	12.40			716.30
1857	15.40			991.00
1858	17.70			896.50
1859	22.00			1725.40

14

Tin	Black(tons)	Stuff(tons)	Tin(tons)	Value(£)
1860	37.60			3130.80
1861	93.30			6985.80
1862	122.20			8075.60
1863	118.00			7858.80
1864	150.10			9687.00
1865	147.70			8536.70
1866	95.50			4739.70
1867	18.60			920.60
1869	64.20			4686.60
1871	38.90			3046.10
1872	35.20			3044.50
1873	21.10			1645.00
1874	22.80			1039.00
1875	12.90			624.50
1877	11.90			442.50
1878	6.30			221.80
1879	11.10			380.20
1880	3.60			161.50
1881	1.70		1.10	90.00
1888	0.60			44.00
1889	1.60			123.00
1890	0.50			33.00
1903	1.80			147.00
1904	7.00			478.00
1905	11.70			941.00
1906	8.80			1087.00
1907	22.60			2564.00
1908	18.10			1291.00
1909	9.50			750.00
1910	15.60			1770.00
1911	21.00			2703.00
1912	14.00			1998.00
1913	8.00			1132.00

Comment 1854 BIRCH TOR; 1862 2 RETURNS AGGREGATED; 1866 NEW
BIRCH TOR & VITIFER; 1867 NEW BIRCH TOR & VITIFER CONSOL;
1869 NEW BIRCH TOR & VITIFER; 1871 NEW BIRCH TOR & VITIFER
CONSOL; 1872 NEW BIRCH TOR & VITIFER; 1873 VALUE EST.; 1874
NEW BIRCH TOR VALUE EST.; 1875 BIRCH TOR; 1877-1881 BIRCH
TOR; 1888 BIRCH TOR

Iron	Ore(tons)	Iron(%)	Value(£)
1906	25.00	58.80	50.00

Comment 1906 HE.

Ownership: 1877-1882 BIRCH TOR MINING CO.; 1883-1902 MOSES BAWDEN; 1903
PHELIPS & PADFIELD; 1904-1913 BIRCH TOR & VITIFER LTD.
Comment 1866-1867 WORKINGS MUCH REDUCED.; 1868-1870 WORKINGS
MUCH REDUCED. NEW BIRCH TOR & VITIFER; 1871-1872 NEW BIRCH
TOR & VITIFER; 1873 NEW BIRCH TOR & VITIFER STOPPED 1873;
1874 NEW BIRCH TOR & VITIFER CONSOLS; 1875-1881 BIRCH TOR;
1882 BIRCH TOR NOT WORKED; 1883 BIRCH TOR; 1884 BIRCH TOR NOT
WORKED IN 1884; 1885 BIRCH TOR NOT WORKED IN 1885; 1886 BIRCH
TOR NOT WORKED IN 1886; 1887 BIRCH TOR NOT WORKING; 1888-1890
BIRCH TOR; 1891 BIRCH TOR SUSPENDED; 1892-1902 BIRCH TOR ONLY

SURFACE WORK OCCAS.
Management: Manager 1868-1869 MOSES BAWDEN; 1870-1876 WM.SKEWIS; 1891
MOSES BAWDEN
Chief Agent 1859-1860 JOHN LEAN & JOHN SYMONS; 1861-1862
JOS.MATTHEWS & JOHN SYMONS; 1863-1867 WM.SKEWIS & JOHN
SYMONS; 1868-1874 W.TREWARTHEN; 1877-1878 MOSES BAWDEN;
1892-1902 MOSES BAWDEN; 1903 JOHN WEBB; 1904-1913
H.M.D.WILLCOCKS
Secretary 1859-1862 JOS.MATTHEWS (P); 1863-1869 WM.SKEWIS;
1870-1876 MOSES BAWDEN; 1879-1890 MOSES BAWDEN

Employment:

	Underground	Surface	Total
1878-1879		3	3
1880		4	4
1881		2	2
1888-1890		2	2
1896-1898		1	1
1903	4	14	18
1904	6	13	19
1905	6	14	20
1906	16	10	26
1907	20	15	35
1908	11	11	22
1909	15	9	24
1910	12	8	20
1911	15	9	24
1912	8	10	18
1913	12	6	18

BIRCH TOR,EAST   NORTH BOVEY   SX 693810 0039

Production: Tin

	Black(tons)	Stuff(tons)	Tin(tons)	Value(£)
1854	5.00			283.00
1863	1.30			87.10
1864	0.80			54.10

Comment 1863 NEW EAST BIRCH TOR
Ownership: Comment 1863-1867 NEW EAST BIRCH TOR
Management: Manager 1860-1862 JOHN LEAN
Chief Agent 1860-1862 JOHN SYMONS; 1863-1867 JOS.MATTHEWS
Secretary 1860-1862 JOS.MATTHEWS (P)

BORRINGTON CONSOLS   PLYMPTON   SX 531584 0040

Production: Lead & Silver

	Ore(tons)	Lead(tons)	Silver(ozs)	Value(£)
1852	32.00	22.00	1300.00	
1853	No detailed return			
1854	228.20	135.00		
1855	130.80	44.20	2122.00	
1856	6.00	3.70	178.00	
1857	No detailed return			

Comment 1852-1857 BORINGDON CONSOLS

BORRINGTON CONSOLS   PLYMPTON   Continued

         Zinc   Ore(tons) Metal(tons)   Value(£)
         1857   8.00   14.40
         Comment 1857 BORRINGDON CONSOLS
         Arsenic   Ore(tons) Metal(tons)   Value(£)
         1855   147.00
         Comment 1855 ARSENICAL MUNDIC

BORRINGTON PARK   PLYMPTON   SX 531584 0041

Production: Lead & Silver   Ore(tons) Lead(tons) Silver(ozs)   Value(£)
         1852   8.00   6.00
         1853   123.00   56.00   3310.00
         1854   163.00   75.00   3750.00
         1855   61.00   12.00   669.00
         1856-1860 No detailed return
         Comment 1852-1860 BORINGDON PARK
Ownership: Comment 1863-1865 SUSPENDED
Management: Secretary 1866 JOHN BAYLY & SON (P)

BORRINGTON,EAST   PLYMPTON   SX 537584 0042

Production: Lead   Ore(tons) Metal(tons)   Value(£)
         1852   12.70   8.20
         1853-1854 No detailed return
         Comment 1852-1854 EAST BORINGDON
Ownership: Comment 1863-1865 SUSPENDED

BOTTLE HILL   PLYMPTON   SX 564587 0043

Production: Copper   Ore(tons) Metal(tons)   Value(£)
         1859   161.00   5.10   438.30
         1873   5.00   0.70   46.60
         1874   11.00   1.60   128.70
         1875   14.00   1.50   119.00
         1876   4.00   0.20   18.00
         Comment 1859 (C); 1873 (C); 1874 (C) OLD BOTTLE HILL;
         1875-1876 (C)
         Tin   Black(tons) Stuff(tons)   Tin(tons)   Value(£)
         1852   18.00
         1853   42.00   2698.70
         1854   49.40   2907.40
         1855   26.80   1601.70
         1856   22.00   1430.60
         1862   10.10   646.10
         1863   24.30   1538.20
         1864   19.10   1170.40
         1865   23.30   1265.80
         1873   11.50   887.70
         1874   4.80   256.30
         1875   6.40   316.00

                                  17

BOTTLE HILL

PLYMPTON   Continued

Tin	Black(tons)	Stuff(tons)	Tin(tons)	Value(£)
1876	3.50			157.60
1881	0.80		0.50	44.00
1882	2.20		1.30	125.00

Comment 1862 PART YEAR ONLY; 1873-1876 OLD BOTTLE HILL;
1881-1882 OLD BOTTLE HILL

Arsenic	Ore(tons)	Metal(tons)	Value(£)
1874	7.80		18.90
1875	5.50		27.50

Comment 1874-1875 OLD BOTTLE HILL

Arsenic Pyrite	Ore(tons)	Value(£)
1876	16.50	15.00

Comment 1876 OLD BOTTLE HILL ARSENICAL MUNDIC

Ownership: 1881-1882 J.W.FARLEY & OTHERS
Comment 1871 OLD BOTTLE HILL & NEW BOTTLE HILL; 1872-1875 OLD
BOTTLE HILL; 1881-1882 OLD BOTTLE HILL

Management: Manager 1860-1864 JOHN EDDY; 1865-1868 JOS.EDDY; 1873-1875
RICH.UNSWORTH
Chief Agent 1871 JOS.EDDY; 1872 JOHN GIFFORD; 1881-1882
J.W.FARLEY
Secretary 1859-1860 ?WATSON & ?CUEL(P); 1861-1868 H.E.CROKER
(P); 1871-1873 JOHN HITCHINS; 1874-1875 JEHU.HITCHINS

Employment:	Underground	Surface	Total
1881	2	2	4
1882	3		3

BOTTLE HILL,EAST   PLYMPTON   SX 568587 0044

Production: Tin	Black(tons)	Stuff(tons)	Tin(tons)	Value(£)
1873	1.40			95.70

Management: Chief Agent 1866 J.THOMAS; 1867-1868 JOS.EDDY; 1869-1870
HY.HILL; 1872-1873 JOS.EDDY
Secretary 1868 H.E.CROKER (P); 1869-1870 C.PEARSE (P);
1872-1873 JOHN HITCHINS

BOVEY TRACEY   BOVEY TRACEY   SX 806810 0045

Production: Iron	Ore(tons)	Iron(%)	Value(£)
1892	48.00		100.00
1893	50.00		100.00

Comment 1892-1893 BH.SHAPTOR MINE?

BOWDEN COMMON   BRENTOR   SX 465819 0046

Production: Manganese	Ore(tons)	Metal(tons)	Value(£)
1875	42.00		48.00
1876	76.00		304.00
1877	13.00		39.00

Comment 1875 30 TONS NOT SOLD; 1876-1877 BAWDEN COMMON
Ownership: Comment 1872-1874 BOWDEN HILL

18

BOWDEN COMMON   BRENTOR   Continued

Management: Manager 1873-1874 JOHN GOLDSWORTHY
            Chief Agent 1875-1881 WM.NEWTON
            Secretary 1873-1881 W.B.COBB

BOWDEN DOWN   BRENTOR   SX 463820 0047

Production: Iron No detailed return
Ownership: 1877 NEWTON,JONES & CO.
Management: Chief Agent 1877 WM.NEWTON

BRADBURY   NORTH MOLTON   0048

Production: Iron No detailed return

BRADSANDS   0049

Production: Iron   Ore(tons)   Iron(%)   Value(£)
            1872   3906.00   976.50
            Comment 1872 BH.

BRATTON FLEMING   PLAISTOW   SS 655370 0050

Production: Manganese   Ore(tons) Metal(tons)   Value(£)
            1873   No detailed return
            Comment 1873 SEE SHERWILL
            Iron   Ore(tons)   Iron(%)   Value(£)
            1873-1874 No detailed return
            Comment 1873-1874 SEE SHERWILL
Ownership: Comment 1873-1878 SEE SHERWILL

BRENT   RATTERY   SX 749631 0051

Production: Iron No detailed return
Ownership: Comment 1863 SUSPENDED
Management: Chief Agent 1864-1865 S.COLLINS

BRIMLEY   MOLLAND   SS 818283 0052

Production: Copper   Ore(tons) Metal(tons)   Value(£)
            1878   1.00   0.10   3.50
            Tin No detailed return
            Iron   Ore(tons)   Iron(%)   Value(£)
            1881   213.90   106.90
            1882   927.00   50.00   232.00
            1883   2175.00   544.00
            1887   1821.00
            1888   2060.00   515.00

	Iron	Ore(tons)	Iron(%)	Value(£)
	1889	3125.00		781.00

Comment 1881-1883 BH.; 1887-1889 BH.

Ownership: 1878-1882 MOLLAND MINING CO.; 1888 MOLLAND MINING CO.;
             1891-1893 MOLLAND MINING CO.
Management: Chief Agent 1878-1879 HY.BOYNS; 1881 JOHN BOYNS; 1888 JOHN
             BRAYLEY; 1891-1893 JOHN BRAYLEY
             Secretary 1880-1882 JOHN HAMPTON (S); 1891-1893 F.E.HAMPTON
             (S)

Employment:	Underground	Surface	Total
1878	6	2	8
1879			
1880	10	2	12
1881		4	4
1882	7	4	11
1888	12	6	18
1891	18	8	26
1892	13	6	19

Comment 1879 SEE MOLLAND

BRINSLEY   0053

Production:	Iron	Ore(tons)	Iron(%)	Value(£)
	1878	500.00		340.00

Comment 1878 BH.RAISED BUT NOT SOLD

BRITISH MANGANESE   MILTON ABBOT   0054

Production: Manganese No detailed return
Ownership: 1884-1887 BRITISH MANGANESE CO.; 1888 C.JOHN SIMS
             Comment 1887 NOT WORKING; 1888 SUSPENDED
Management: Chief Agent 1884-1888 WM.PHILLIPS

Employment:	Underground	Surface	Total
1884	6		6
1885-1886	4		4

BRIXHAM   BRIXHAM   0055

Production:	Iron	Ore(tons)	Iron(%)	Value(£)
	1858	1400.00		665.00
	1859	2285.00		1100.00
	1860	2400.00		960.00
	1861	5257.00		2102.80
	1862	3500.00		2040.00
	1863	7014.00		1841.20
	1864	9768.00		4634.00
	1865	16710.00		5527.80
	1866	20005.30		6283.80
	1867	8762.50		2687.40
	1868	3563.80		1069.20

20

Iron	Ore(tons)	Iron(%)	Value(£)
1869	6092.20		1827.30
1870	6100.60		1830.00
1871	8772.70		2631.80
1872	1593.00		477.90
1873	600.00		450.00
1874	2166.00		1025.00
1875	907.50		453.70
1876	1603.00		801.50
1880	462.00		354.00
1898	2990.00		
1899	600.00		
1900	176.00		
1902	100.00	52.00	
1909	676.00		193.00
1910	1038.00	50.00	571.00
1911	160.00	50.50	100.00
1912	150.00	50.50	90.00
1913	20.00	50.00	14.00

Comment 1858 BH.; 1859 BH.INC 85 TONS IRON PAINT; 1860-1861
BH. SHARKHAM POINT; 1862 BH.SHARHAM POINT BRIXHAM&SUND.; 1863
BH.BRIXHAM INN MINES; 1864 BH.; 1865-1867 BH.TWO RETURNS
AGG.; 1868 BH.; 1869-1870 BH.TWO RETURNS AGG.; 1871-1876 BH.;
1880 BH.USED IN COLOUR WORKS; 1898-1900 BH.; 1902 BH.;
1909-1913 BH.

Ownership: 1863 WM.BROWNE; 1871-1872 WELSH IRON WORKS; 1873 P.COOKSON &
CO.; 1875-1876 WM.BROWNE & SONS; 1897 E.H.BAYLDON; 1898-1899
E.H.BAYLDON & STRUHEN; 1900-1912 E.H.BAYLDON; 1913 EXEC.OF
E.H.BAYLDON
Comment 1863 BRIXHAM IRON; 1905-1906 SUSPENDED; 1913
RECOMMENCED JAN.1912

Management: Chief Agent 1863 WM.GROSE; 1871-1873 W.H.HOSKING; 1875-1876
WM.BROWNE; 1897-1904 W.A.GROSE; 1905-1908 D.H.BAYLDON;
1909-1913 A.S.HUGHES
Secretary 1905-1909 D.H.BAYLDON; 1910-1912 G.A.HIGLETT

Employment:

	Underground	Surface	Total
1897	20	9	29
1898	25	6	31
1900	10	6	16
1901	19	1	20
1902	8	4	12
1903-1906		1	1
1907	3	5	8
1908	5		5
1909	2	2	4
1910-1911		8	8
1912	3	3	6
1913	2	2	4

Production: Iron

	Ore(tons)	Iron(%)	Value(£)
1872	400.00		240.00

Comment 1872 HE.
Ownership: 1870-1872 VAN IRON ORE CO.
Management: Chief Agent 1870-1872 W.H.HOSKING

BROOKWOOD   BUCKFASTLEIGH   SX 718675 0057

Production: Copper

	Ore(tons)	Metal(tons)	Value(£)
1861	269.00	17.70	1561.90
1862	699.00	48.40	3930.10
1863	971.00	58.60	4443.70
1864	899.00	45.90	3696.50
1865	1381.00	69.80	5319.90
1866	1557.00	98.80	6450.00
1867	1689.00	102.10	7056.30
1868	1208.00	70.60	4672.30
1869	241.00	10.00	557.80
1870	1435.00	109.10	6577.00
1871	1719.00	123.60	7685.80
1872	1775.00	138.40	11164.10
1873	1928.00	146.20	9730.30
1874	1776.00	132.30	8615.30
1875	1512.00	97.00	7152.90
1876	1081.00	68.50	4547.60
1877	579.10	38.30	2525.40

Comment 1861-1876 (C)
Ownership: 1876-1877 BROOKWOOD MINING CO.; 1878-1879 SOUTH DEVON UNITED
MINE CO.
Comment 1880-1881 SEE SOUTH DEVON UNITED
Management: Manager 1860-1863 S.ROBBINS; 1869-1879 THOS.TREVELYAN
Chief Agent 1864-1865 G.HOSKINS; 1866-1868 THOS.TREVELYAN;
1869-1871 WM.HOSKINS; 1872-1874 WM.HOOPER; 1875-1879 JOHN
MORCOM
Secretary 1860-1863 HY.CREASE (P); 1866-1879 JOHN CLARK
ISAACS

BROOKWOOD,EAST   BUCKFASTLEIGH   SX 717684 0058

Production: Copper No detailed return
            Tin No detailed return
Ownership: Comment 1874-1875 INC.BURCHETTS
Management: Chief Agent 1864-1867 J.BENNETT
Secretary 1866-1867 ?HATHERLEY; 1874-1875 GEO.SPARK

BROOKWOOD,NEW   BUCKFASTLEIGH   SX 721678 0059

Production: Copper No detailed return
Ownership: 1884-1885 NEW BROOKWOOD MINING CO.; 1888-1892 J.A.TRENCHARD
Comment 1885 NOT WORKED IN 1885; 1889-1892 SUSPENDED

BROOKWOOD,NEW   BUCKFASTLEIGH   Continued

Management: Chief Agent 1884-1885 JAS.BROWNING; 1888-1892 JAS.BROWNING
Employment: Underground   Surface   Total
               1884   4   2   6
               1888   8   2   10
               1889   10   10
               1891   1   1

BULKAMORE   RATTERY   SX 749631 0060

Production: Iron   Ore(tons)   Iron(%)   Value(£)
               1874   1000.00   750.00
               1875   3400.00   3050.00
            Comment 1874-1875 BH.
Ownership: 1874 BULKAMORE MAGNETIC IRON CO.; 1875-1876 BULKAMORE
            MAGNETIC IRON CO.LTD.
Management: Manager 1874 E.COOPER & CO.
            Chief Agent 1875-1876 T.GEO.DUGARD

⚹ BULLER AND BERTHA   BUCKLAND MONACHORUM   SX 487696 0061 ⚹

Production: Copper No detailed return
Ownership: Comment 1862-1865 SUSPENDED
Management: Manager 1859 F.FOOT; 1860 THOS.FOOT; 1861 T.FOOT JNR.
            Chief Agent 1859-1861 F.FOOT JNR.
            Secretary 1859-1863 JAS.WOLFERSTAN (P)

BURCHETTS   BUCKFASTLEIGH   SX 722679 0062

Production: Copper No detailed return
Ownership: Comment 1874-1875 SEE EAST BROOKWOOD

BUZZACOTT   COMBE MARTIN   0063

Production: Lead & Silver No detailed return
Management: Manager 1873-1876 SML.MITCHELL
            Secretary 1873 JOB.PEARSON; 1874-1876 JOHN PEARSON

CALLEYS IRON PAINT   BRIXHAM   0064

Production: Iron No detailed return
Ownership: 1864-1865 SML.CALLEY

CALSTOCK CONSOLS   CALSTOCK,CORNWALL   SX 426696 0065

Production: Copper   Ore(tons) Metal(tons)   Value(£)
               1856   328.00   18.90   1609.50
               1857   175.00   12.30   1126.10

23

CALSTOCK CONSOLS   CALSTOCK,CORNWALL   Continued

          Copper   Ore(tons) Metal(tons)   Value(£)
          1858   686.00   43.90   3984.00
          Comment 1856-1858 (C)

CARDWELL   LAMERTON   SX 433797 0066

Production: Manganese   Ore(tons) Metal(tons)   Value(£)
          1868   No detailed return
          Comment 1868 SEE CHILLATON
Ownership: 1868-1870 C.JOHN SIMS (P)
Management: Manager 1868-1870 C.JOHN SIMS & F.SIMS
          Secretary 1868-1870 F.SIMS (P)

CARPENTER   SYDENHAM DAMEREL   SX 414766 0067

Production: Lead & Silver   Ore(tons) Lead(tons) Silver(ozs) Value(£)
          1855   57.00   43.00   782.00
          1856   36.60   21.60   835.00
          1857-1860 No detailed return
          Comment 1856 AG INC.4 OTHER MINES
          Zinc   Ore(tons) Metal(tons)   Value(£)
          1854   80.00
          1855   No detailed return
          1856   55.30   119.00
          Comment 1855 SEE GREAT WHEAL BADDERN,CORNWALL

CAWSAND VALE   0068

Production: Copper   Ore(tons) Metal(tons)   Value(£)
          1868   120.00   6.70   410.10
          1869   98.00   5.70   376.60
          Comment 1868 (C); 1869 (S)

CHAGFORD   CHAGFORD   0069

Production: Tin   Black(tons) Stuff(tons)   Tin(tons)   Value(£)
          1872   2.50   206.40
          1873   0.80   60.00

CHALLACOMBE   CHALLACOMBE   SS 593476 0070

Production: Lead No detailed return
          Iron   Ore(tons)   Iron(%)   Value(£)
          1873   50.00   37.50
          Comment 1873 BH.
Ownership: 1873-1874 J.CARTER

                                   24

CHALLACOMBE,WEST   COMBE MARTIN   SS 585473 0071

Production: Lead & Silver No detailed return
            Iron No detailed return
Ownership: Comment 1864-1865 SEE NEW COMBE MARTIN
Management: Chief Agent 1874 JOHN TREWEEKE; 1875-1876 JOHN TREWEEKE &
            WM.SIMS
            Secretary 1874-1876 T.CARTER

 CHILLATON   MILTON ABBOT   SX 431812 0072

Production: Manganese	Ore(tons)	Metal(tons)	Value(£)
1858	1400.00		
1859	1056.00		3168.00
1860	832.00		2796.00
1867	769.50		
1868	1700.00		7650.00
1870	4815.50		19396.80
1871	5453.90		22685.50
1872	7681.00		38405.00
1873	8254.90		55184.00
1874	5054.50		25272.50
1875	2754.40		13770.00
1876	2430.90		8200.00
1877	2159.00		5397.00
1878	1000.00		2000.00
1879	400.00		800.00
1880	800.00		2400.00
1881	1224.00		4284.00
1882	782.00		2737.00
1883	780.00		2000.00
1884	535.00		1000.00
1885	348.00		
1886	160.00		320.00
1887	240.00		300.00
1888	No detailed return		
1890	183.00		198.00
1891	130.00		181.00
1892	840.00		1050.00
1893	325.00		220.00
1894	31.00		12.00
1895	387.00		145.00
1902	120.00		100.00
1903	15.00		12.00
1904	177.00		142.00
1905	122.00		139.00
1906	24.00		21.00
1907	34.00		34.00

            Comment 1858 CHILLATON MANOR MINES + 5MINES; 1859-1860
            CHILLATON MANOR MINES + 4MINES; 1867 INC.3 OTHER MINES; 1868
            INC.5 OTHER MINES; 1870-1872 INC.HOGSTOR; 1873-1874
            INC.HOGSTOR ETC.; 1875-1887 INC.HOGSTOR; 1888 INC.HOGSTOR,
            SUSPENDED; 1890-1895 INC.HOGSTOR; 1902-1907 INC.HOGSTOR
Ownership: 1868-1872 C.JOHN SIMS (P); 1877-1887 SIMS BROS.; 1890 JOHN

BABBAGE; 1891-1895 CHILLATON MANGANESE CO.LTD.; 1901-1909
JAS.A.JOBLING
Comment 1872-1878 INC.HOGSTOR; 1880-1887 INC.HOGSTOR; 1890
INC.HOGSTOR; 1895 IN LIQUIDATION; 1901-1908 INC.HOGSTOR; 1909
INC.HOGSTOR ABANDONED JUNE 1909
Management: Manager 1860-1867 JOHN SIMS; 1868-1872 C.JOHN SIMS & F.SIMS;
1873-1875 WM.DOIDGE; 1876-1880 HY.SIMS; 1881 JAS.B.PROUT
Chief Agent 1860-1867 N.TRUSCOTT; 1873 W.WHITE; 1874-1875
M.WHITE; 1876-1880 WM.DOIDGE; 1881 ED.BRIMACOMBE; 1891-1895
JOHN GOLDSWORTHY; 1901-1908 WM.GILL; 1909 WM.ARMSTRONG JNR.
Secretary 1860-1867 JOHN SIMS (P); 1868-1872 F.SIMS (P);
1873-1885 SIMS BROS.; 1886-1887 HY.SIMS; 1890 JOHN BABBAGE;
1891-1895 WM.TIDBOALD (S)

Employment:	Underground	Surface	Total
1878	6	20	26
1879	13	26	39
1880	17	27	44
1881	19	39	58
1882	19	40	59
1883	26	35	61
1884	8	9	17
1885	16	16	32
1886	9	11	20
1890		7	7
1891	16	16	32
1892	22	18	40
1893	2	14	16
1894		9	9
1895	4	5	9
1901	9	5	14
1902	6	5	11
1903	10	5	15
1904	9	5	14
1905	4		4
1906	5		5
1907		6	6
1908		9	9
1909	10		10

Comment 1878 INC.HOGSTOR; 1880-1886 INC.HOGSTOR; 1890
INC.HOGSTOR; 1901-1909 INC.HOGSTOR

✳ CHILLATON,EAST   MILTON ABBOT   SX 465819 0073✳

Production: Manganese No detailed return
Ownership: 1880-1881 THE ATWAY MANGANESE CO.
           Comment 1880-1881 INC.ATWAY

CHINTER   BRIXHAM   0074

Production: Iron	Ore(tons)	Iron(%)	Value(£)
1865	No detailed return		

BRIXHAM

```
              Iron              Ore(tons)    Iron(%)    Value(£)
              1866              1524.00
              1872       No detailed return
              Comment 1865 BH.SEE SHARKHAM; 1866 BH.FOR VALUE SEE DREWS;
              1872 BH.SEE TORBAY IRON
Ownership:    1863 WM.BROWNE; 1864 SML.CALLEY; 1865-1866 WM.BROWNE
              Comment 1872-1874 SEE TORBAY IRON
Management:   Chief Agent 1863 PHAR.GROSE; 1864 S.COLLINS; 1865-1866
              PHAR.GROSE
```

CHURSTON   CHURSTON FERRERS   0075

```
Production:  Iron No detailed return
Ownership:   1864 ED.PRIOR & CO.; 1865 WM.BROWNE
             Comment 1865 SUSPENDED
Management:  Chief Agent 1864 ED.PRIOR
```

✳ CLINTON   MILTON ABBOT   0076 ✳

```
Production:  Manganese No detailed return
Ownership:   Comment 1860-1862 CLINTON AND EDGECUMBE UNITED; 1863-1865
             CLINTON & EDGECUMBE UNITED SUSPENDED
```

✳ COLCHARTON   TAVISTOCK   SX 450730 0077 ✳

```
Production:  Copper No detailed return
             Iron No detailed return
Ownership:   1872-1873 THOS.MORRIS (P)
             Comment 1873 STOPPED 1873
Management:  Manager 1872-1873 JAS.& IS.RICHARDS
             Chief Agent 1872 WM.WOOLCOCK & WM.CLEMO; 1873 HY.GEORGE &
             HY.RODDA
             Secretary 1872-1873 ALEX.ALLEN (S)
```

✳ COLLACOMBE   SYDENHAM DAMEREL   SX 433771 0078 ✳

```
Production:  Zinc             Ore(tons) Metal(tons)    Value(£)
             1858              57.30                    172.00
             1859             124.90                    368.80
             1860             103.40                    298.10
             1861              50.80                    110.50
             1862              25.50                     41.40
             1863              24.10                     72.00
             1864              59.00                    132.60
             1865              35.80                     92.10
             1868       No detailed return
             Comment 1864 COLLOCOMBE; 1868 SEE COLLACOMBE CORNWALL
             Copper           Ore(tons) Metal(tons)    Value(£)
             1855             213.00      14.80        1559.00
```

27

COLLACOMBE   SYDENHAM DAMEREL

Continued

Copper	Ore(tons)	Metal(tons)	Value(£)
1856	1570.00	100.20	9140.70
1857	1866.00	120.90	11834.70
1858	1168.00	74.70	6545.10
1859	1228.00	77.20	6984.90
1860	1146.00	59.00	4989.60
1861	694.00	40.00	3334.30
1862	47.00	2.50	192.80
1863	112.00	4.70	320.10
1864	117.00	5.80	464.90
1865	121.00	4.50	315.80
1866	50.00	2.10	162.30
1867	39.00	1.50	94.80
1868	49.00	2.40	161.10
1869	56.00	1.80	80.70
1884	21.00		60.00
1885	5.00		15.00

Comment 1855-1869 (C); 1884-1885 COLLACOMBE CONSOLS
Ownership: 1883-1885 COLLACOMBE CONSOLS MINING CO.
Comment 1862 SUSPENDED; 1883-1885 COLLACOMBE CONSOLS
Management: Manager 1860-1861 JAS.RICHARDS
Chief Agent 1859 JAS.RICHARDS & SML.MITCHELL; 1863
JAS.RICHARDS; 1864-1865 SML.MITCHELL; 1883-1885 WM.SKEWIS
Secretary 1859-1865 THOS.MORRIS (P)

Employment:	Underground	Surface	Total
1883	22	22	44
1884	17	2	19
1885	15	9	24

COLLACOMBE,WEST   SYDENHAM DAMEREL   SX 414766 0079

Production: Lead & Silver	Ore(tons)	Lead(tons)	Silver(ozs)	Value(£)
1856	11.00	6.00	120.00	
1857	10.30	7.50		

Zinc	Ore(tons)	Metal(tons)	Value(£)
1856	99.60		241.40
1857	37.00		120.30

Copper	Ore(tons)	Metal(tons)	Value(£)
1856	256.00	14.00	1222.00

Comment 1856 (C)
Ownership: Comment 1862-1865 SUSPENDED
Management: Chief Agent 1860-1861 SML.MITCHELL

COMBE MARTIN   COMBE MARTIN   SS 588465 0080

Production: Lead & Silver	Ore(tons)	Lead(tons)	Silver(ozs)	Value(£)
1845	174.00	104.00		
1846	213.00	127.00		
1847	202.00	121.00		
1877	3.30	2.40	48.00	50.00
1879	2.90	2.20	40.00	32.20

28

```
                Comment 1845-1847 COMBMARTIN
Ownership:      1876-1880 COMBE MARTIN MINING CO.
                Comment 1880 OLD COMBE MARTIN ABAND.OCT.1880
Management:     Manager 1876 EDW.HOSKING; 1880 JOHN HARRIS
                Chief Agent 1873 JOHN TREWEEKE; 1876 CHAS.H.MAUNDER; 1877
                JOHN COMER & CHAS.H.MAUNDER; 1878 JOHN HARRIS; 1879 JOHN
                COMER
                Secretary 1873 F.W.DARBY (S); 1876-1879 JAS.WATSON (S)
```

Employment:	Underground	Surface	Total
1878	12		12
1879	16	4	20
1880	15		15
1882	3	1	4

COMBE MARTIN,NEW   COMBE MARTIN   SS 585473 0081

```
Production: Lead & Silver No detailed return
Ownership:  Comment 1864-1865 LATE WEST CHALLACOMBE
Management: Secretary 1864-1865 G.T.GOODMAN
```

COMBE MARTIN,WEST   COMBE MARTIN   SS 585473 0082

```
Production: Lead No detailed return
Ownership:  1875-1881 WEST COMBE MARTIN SILVER LEAD MINE CO.
            Comment 1879-1881 NOT WORKED
Management: Chief Agent 1875 S.MATTHEWS & JOHN TREWEEKE; 1876 JOHN
            TREWEEKE; 1877 W.H.HOSKING & JOHN TREWEEKE; 1878-1880 JOHN
            TREWEEKE; 1881 JOHN COMER
            Secretary 1875-1878 FRED.THOMAS (S)
```

Employment:	Underground	Surface	Total
1878	4		4

COMBE,NORTH   LUSTLEIGH   0083

```
Production: Iron No detailed return
Ownership:  1895 P.J.DICK
Management: Chief Agent 1895 A.LIVINGSTONE
```

COMFORT   BRAUNTON   0084

```
Production: Manganese No detailed return
Management: Chief Agent 1876-1877 JOS.POPE
            Secretary 1876-1877 JOS.POPE
```

CONCORD   SYDENHAM DAMEREL   SX 427770 0085

Production:	Ore(tons)	Lead(tons)	Silver(ozs)	Value(£)
1862	5.10	3.20	65.00	

CONCORD   SYDENHAM DAMEREL   Continued

```
              Copper No detailed return
Ownership:    Comment 1865 SUSPENDED
Management:   Manager 1860 Z.WILLIAMS; 1861-1863 Z.WILLIAMS & E.S.CODD;
              1864 THOS.FOOT
              Chief Agent 1860-1863 H.LUKE; 1864 WM.SNELL
              Secretary 1860-1861 W.S.TROTTER (P); 1864-1865 GEO.DOWN
```

COOMBE   SOUTH MOLTON   SS 701285 0086

```
Production:   Lead & Silver No detailed return
Management:   Chief Agent 1874-1878 W.F.WHITE
              Secretary 1873-1878 W.T.ENGLEDUE
```

✳ CORYTON   CORYTON   SX 477851 0087 ✳

Production: Manganese	Ore(tons)	Metal(tons)	Value(£)
1858	No detailed return		
1859	175.00		525.00
1860	100.00		300.00
1888	156.00		195.00

```
              Comment 1858 SEE CHILLATON
Ownership:    1882-1888 HY.MARTIN; 1889 THOS.H.NEWMAN
              Comment 1889 SUSPENDED
Management:   Chief Agent 1882-1888 WM.HOOPER; 1889 JEFF.MICHELMORE
```

Employment:	Underground	Surface	Total
1882-1884	6		6
1885	6	6	12
1886	6	9	15
1887		2	2
1888		3	3

COT QUARRY   SHIRWELL   SS 607384 0088

Production: Manganese	Ore(tons)	Metal(tons)	Value(£)
1874	50.00		250.00

```
Management:   Manager 1874-1875 J.TRESIDDER
              Chief Agent 1874 T.PLINT
              Secretary 1874-1875 R.DAWSON CLEGG
```

COUNTESBURY   COUNTISBURY   0089

```
Production:   Iron No detailed return
Management:   Chief Agent 1874 JOHN COMER
```

✳ COURTENAY   TAVISTOCK   0090 ✳

```
Production:   Copper No detailed return
Management:   Manager 1869-1870 WM.RICHARDS
```

Secretary 1869-1870 WM.RICHARDS (P)

✳ CREBOR   TAVISTOCK   SX 460724 0091 ✳

Production: Copper

Year	Ore(tons)	Metal(tons)	Value(£)
1852	209.00	15.70	1344.80
1853	438.00	32.30	3261.90
1854	351.00	19.70	1887.80
1855	483.00	24.10	2306.10
1856	244.00	9.60	759.60
1859	151.00	5.80	480.30
1862	195.00	9.70	755.10
1863	346.00	17.50	1288.40
1864	487.00	27.80	2244.30
1865	519.00	29.20	2211.70
1866	456.00	24.10	1499.00
1867	228.00	12.70	856.00
1868	322.00	18.40	1153.90
1869	296.00	17.50	1025.10
1870	372.00	23.70	1284.40
1871	398.00	23.60	1290.40
1872	192.50	11.80	828.60
1872	557.50	30.90	2136.90
1872	365.00	19.10	1308.30
1873	462.00	26.40	1470.10
1874	597.00	44.60	2958.70
1875	482.00	30.60	2207.30
1876	824.00	50.60	3166.60
1877	1037.00	50.40	2759.60
1878	788.00	42.10	2019.60
1879	1183.00	80.00	4482.30
1880	2885.40	216.40	11656.90
1881	2879.70	190.80	9271.10
1882	2849.60	171.00	9973.00
1883	2526.30	189.50	9698.00
1884	2924.00		8020.00
1885	3024.00		7695.00
1886	2562.00		4707.00
1887	564.00		1142.00
1888	1286.00		4308.00
1889	952.00		2278.00
1890	616.00		2153.00
1891	310.00		1139.00
1892	134.00		447.00
1893	45.00		184.00

Comment 1852-1856 (C); 1859 (C); 1862-1872 (C); 1872 (P)
COPPER EST.; 1872 1872 TOTAL; 1873-1876 (C)

Tin	Black(tons)	Stuff(tons)	Tin(tons)	Value(£)
1887	0.80	60.00		37.00
1888	No detailed return			
1889	12.00	1117.00		594.00

Arsenic No detailed return

Arsenic Pyrite	Ore(tons)	Value(£)
1869	84.00	68.80
1874	190.30	149.00
1875	370.00	402.00
1877	198.90	38.00
1878	209.50	162.40
1879	258.60	139.30
1880	413.80	375.90
1881	509.60	459.50
1887	2500.00	1800.00
1888	1958.00	1546.00
1889	2985.00	2397.00
1890	2008.00	1518.00
1891	1615.00	1775.00
1892	1845.00	2373.00
1893	1733.00	2060.00
1894	1501.00	2179.00
1895	1374.00	1845.00
1896	1404.00	2201.00
1897	884.00	1180.00
1898	1094.00	1816.00
1899	703.00	1488.00
1900	542.00	1454.00
1901	244.00	561.00
1902	294.00	453.00

Comment 1877 ARSENICAL MUNDIC

Ownership: 1877-1890 WHEAL CREBOR MINING CO.; 1891-1904 WHEAL CREBOR
CO.; 1908 DUKE OF BEDFORD
Comment 1880-1881 THE OLD CROWNDALE; 1903-1904 SUSPENDED

Management: Manager 1859-1867 JOHN GIFFORD; 1868 JNO.GIFFORD; 1873-1874
JOHN GOLDSWORTHY; 1875-1879 JOHN ANDREWS; 1881 GEO.ROWE;
1891-1893 MOSES BAWDEN (P)
Chief Agent 1864-1867 JOHN HITCHINS; 1869-1871 JOHN
GOLDSWORTHY; 1872 JNO.GOLDSWORTHY; 1874-1876 JOHN ANDREWS;
1880 GEO.ROWE & MOSES BAWDEN; 1881 MOSES BAWDEN; 1891-1904
P.D.HOLMAN; 1908 T.S.BLISS
Secretary 1859-1863 H.E.CROKER (P); 1864-1867 H.E.CROKER;
1868-1873 JOHN HITCHINS; 1874-1875 JEHU.HITCHINS; 1876-1881
C.B.PARRY (S); 1882-1890 MOSES BAWDEN; 1891-1893 C.B.PARRY
(S); 1894-1904 MOSES BAWDEN

Employment:	Underground	Surface	Total
1878	36	21	57
1879	63	41	104
1880	70	63	133
1881	102	83	185
1882	58	60	118
1883	70	61	131
1884	65	76	141
1885	60	49	109
1886	56	52	108
1887	53	35	88
1888	77	52	129
1889	28	34	62

	Underground	Surface	Total
1890	37	37	74
1891	30	24	54
1892	31	30	61
1893	33	25	58
1894	22	25	47
1895	24	22	46
1896	18	18	36
1897	11	9	20
1898	14	10	24
1900	11	7	18
1901	11	5	16
1902	5	7	12
1908		3	3

✸ CREBOR,EAST   TAVISTOCK   SX 478726 0092 ✸

Production: Copper   Ore(tons) Metal(tons)   Value(£)
            1881   120.00   9.50   510.60
            Arsenic Pyrite Ore(tons)   Value(£)
            1881   33.00   29.80
Ownership: 1879-1881 EAST CREBOR MINING CO.
Management: Manager 1879-1881 GEO.ROWE
            Secretary 1879-1881 H.L.PHILLIPS
Employment: Underground   Surface   Total
            1879   10   10
            1880   15   15   30
            1881   17   5   22

✸ CREBOR,SOUTH   TAVISTOCK   SX 464714 0093 ✸

Production: Copper No detailed return
Ownership: 1880-1881 SOUTH WHEAL CREBOR LTD.; 1882-1883 SOUTH CREBOR
            MINING CO.
            Comment 1882 NOT WORKED
Management: Chief Agent 1880-1883 JOHN GOLDSWORTHY
Employment: Underground   Surface   Total
            1880   19   9   28
            1881   16   5   21
            1883   8   5   13

✸ CREBOR,WEST   TAVISTOCK   SX 452721 0094 ✸

Production: Copper   Ore(tons) Metal(tons)   Value(£)
            1885   19.00   24.00
Ownership: 1880-1885 WEST CREBOR MINING CO.
Management: Chief Agent 1880-1885 JOHN ANDREWS
Employment: Underground   Surface   Total
            1880   9   6   15
            1881   18   8   26

33

CREBOR,WEST   TAVISTOCK   Continued

	Underground	Surface	Total
1882	12	5	17
1883	14	6	20
1884	12	4	16
1885	12	3	15

 CRELAKE   TAVISTOCK   SX 478736 0095

Production: Lead & Silver

Lead & Silver	Ore(tons)	Lead(tons)	Silver(ozs)	Value(£)
1860	30.00	22.00	308.00	
1861	220.00	163.00	1956.00	
1862	245.00	183.00	2750.00	
1863	340.00	251.60	3765.00	
1864	254.00	182.00	3360.00	
1865	69.10	44.70	892.00	
1866	9.70	5.70	115.00	

Copper	Ore(tons)	Metal(tons)	Value(£)
1859	459.00	36.70	3509.90
1860	1243.00	83.50	7430.20
1861	2156.00	149.70	12923.80
1862	2014.00	110.80	8347.10
1863	712.00	36.60	2575.70
1864	339.00	10.20	645.00
1865	140.00	5.90	440.20
1866	340.00	16.30	1029.80
1867	711.00	40.70	2928.30
1868	1344.00	69.80	4517.90
1869	1369.00	67.60	4093.80
1870	677.00	30.60	1729.30
1871	64.00	2.40	136.00
1872	22.70	0.80	59.50
1874	16.00	1.10	73.20

Comment 1859-1871 (C); 1872 (P) COPPER EST.; 1874 (C)

Arsenic Pyrite	Ore(tons)	Value(£)
1869	2099.00	2185.40
1870	1243.60	1235.80
1871	1504.20	1060.00
1874	376.00	235.60

Ownership: Comment 1866-1870 WORKINGS GREATLY REDUCED
Management: Manager 1859 WM.SKEWIS
             Chief Agent 1860-1861 WM.SKEWIS; 1862-1870 WM.SKEWIS &
             H.HOOPER
             Secretary 1859-1860 JOHN BAYLY (P); 1861-1866 JOHN BAYLY &
             SON (P); 1867-1870 MOSES BAWDEN

CROWNDALE   TAVISTOCK   SX 470725 0096

Production: Copper

Copper	Ore(tons)	Metal(tons)	Value(£)
1858	322.00	15.60	1319.70
1859	186.00	7.00	617.60
1862	44.00	1.00	59.90

34

Copper	Ore(tons)	Metal(tons)	Value(£)
1874	10.00	0.40	25.50

Comment 1858-1859 (C); 1862 (C); 1874 (C) NEW CROWNDALE

Tin	Black(tons)	Stuff(tons)	Tin(tons)	Value(£)
1875	3.30			136.10

Comment 1875 NEW CROWNDALE

Arsenic Pyrite	Ore(tons)	Value(£)
1870	30.00	18.80
1871	28.00	27.30

Ownership: Comment 1874-1875 NEW CROWNDALE; 1880-1881 SEE CREBOR
Management: Manager 1875 JAS.MURRAY
              Chief Agent 1859-1865 JAS.RICHARDS; 1874 ROBT.TOYE; 1875
              JAS.MURRAY
              Secretary 1859-1865 THOS.MORRIS (P); 1875 JACOB LEGASSICK

✳ CROWNDALE,EAST   TAVISTOCK   SX 478726 0097 ✳

Production: Copper

Copper	Ore(tons)	Metal(tons)	Value(£)
1852	72.00	7.50	719.30
1853	286.00	22.80	2209.10
1854	247.00	16.60	1665.70
1869	3.00	0.10	5.40

Comment 1852-1854 (C); 1869 (C)
Ownership: 1880 EAST CROWNDALE MINING CO.
Management: Manager 1880 HY.TREGANOWAN

Employment:

	Underground	Surface	Total
1880	1		1

CWM MOLTON   SOUTH MOLTON   SS 701285 0098

Production: Lead & Silver

	Ore(tons)	Lead(tons)	Silver(ozs)	Value(£)
1874	7.80	5.50	36.00	

✳ DARTMOOR,NORTH   LYDFORD   SX 559858 0099 ✳

Production: Tin

	Black(tons)	Stuff(tons)	Tin(tons)	Value(£)
1864	1.20			70.40
1865	1.90			75.70

Comment 1864 NORTH DARTMOOR STREAMS
Management: Manager 1872 F.SIMS
              Chief Agent 1872 JOHN FARLEY; 1873 JOHN SYMONS
              Secretary 1872 C.JOHN SIMS; 1873 W.T.ENGLEDEW

DEAN PRIOR   DEAN PRIOR   SX 729657 0100

Production: Tin No detailed return
Ownership: 1877-1878 SIR GEO.ELLIOT
              Comment 1875 DEAN
Management: Manager 1875-1877 SML.LAKE

Chief Agent 1878 E.S.FORD
Secretary 1875-1876 SIR GEO.ELLIOT
Employment: Underground   Surface   Total
          1878   10   2   12

DEVON   0101

Production: Copper   Ore(tons) Metal(tons)   Value(£)
            1865   4.00   0.10   8.20
            Comment 1865 (C)

✳ DEVON AND BEDFORD,GREAT   TAVISTOCK   SX 450730 0102 ✳

Production: Copper No detailed return
Management: Manager 1866 WM.SKEWIS
            Chief Agent 1862-1863 GEO.RICHARDS; 1864-1866 JAS.RICHARDS
            Secretary 1864-1866 GEO.DOWN

✳ DEVON AND CORNWALL UNITED   TAVISTOCK   SX 463701 0104 ✳

Production: Copper   Ore(tons) Metal(tons)   Value(£)
            1852   98.00   5.80   475.80
            1855   341.00   13.70   1256.50
            1856-1861 No detailed return
            1862   1205.00   58.20   4357.30
            1863   1680.00   69.80   4800.10
            1864   1643.00   84.50   6704.70
            1865   2920.00   135.30   9912.90
            1866   1843.00   88.40   5406.50
            1867   1155.00   61.10   4167.90
            1868   549.00   30.50   1955.70
            1869   42.00   1.80   97.60
            1870   172.00   9.20   511.20
            1871   57.00   2.80   161.20
            Comment 1852 (C); 1855 (C) DEVON & CORNWALL; 1856-1861 SEE
            DEVON & CORNWALL UNITED,CORNWALL; 1862-1871 (C) DEVON &
            CORNWALL
Management: Manager 1859-1867 THOS.NEILL
            Chief Agent 1859-1867 THOS.HORSWILL; 1868 JAS.DONNAL &
            ED.JAMES; 1869-1870 ED.JAMES
            Secretary 1859-1867 GEO.DOWN (P); 1868-1870 T.J.HAMBLY

✳ DEVON AND COURTENAY   WHITCHURCH   SX 472717 0105 ✳

Production: Lead   Ore(tons) Metal(tons)   Value(£)
            1859   2.80   1.90
            1860   No detailed return
            Copper   Ore(tons) Metal(tons)   Value(£)
            1852   70.00   6.50   570.20

36

Copper	Ore(tons)	Metal(tons)	Value(£)
1853	81.00	5.70	627.00
1854	196.00	17.40	1819.00
1855	134.00	8.30	840.90
1856	200.00	11.30	1028.10
1857	276.00	13.10	1311.70
1858	178.00	9.70	869.00
1859	186.00	9.00	834.00
1860	167.00	7.10	597.60
1862	22.00	0.70	48.40
1869	25.00	2.10	140.60
1877	198.90	14.80	915.50
1878	41.70	2.50	123.10

Comment 1852-1858 (C) DEVON & COURTNEY; 1859 (C) DEVON &
COURTENEY; 1860 (C); 1862 (C); 1869 (C) COURTENAY; 1877 (C)
COURTNEY; 1878 (C) COURTENAY

Ownership: 1876 COURTNEY CO.; 1877 WHEAL COURTENAY CO.; 1878 JAS.B.PROUT
& JOHN GOLDSWORTHY
Comment 1862-1865 SUSPENDED; 1868-1869 COURTNEY; 1870
COURTENAY; 1876-1877 COURTNEY; 1878-1879 COURTENAY

Management: Manager 1859-1861 THOS.BAWDEN; 1868-1870 JNO.GIFFORD
Chief Agent 1868-1870 JOHN HITCHINS (S); 1876-1877 JOHN
GOLDSWORTHY; 1878-1879 JAS.B.PROUT
Secretary 1859-1865 H.E.CROKER (P); 1868-1870 H.E.CROKER (P);
1878-1879 JOHN GOLDSWORTHY

Employment: | | Underground | Surface | Total |
|---|---|---|---|
| 1878 | 5 | 4 | 9 |

✳ DEVON BULLER BUCKLAND MONACHORUM SX 500671 0106 ✳

Production: Copper

	Ore(tons)	Metal(tons)	Value(£)
1855	87.00	6.20	614.70
1856	189.00	13.20	1168.80
1857	327.00	21.30	2081.40
1858	204.00	11.70	1012.90
1859	203.00	13.20	1182.50
1860	111.00	7.00	615.60

Comment 1855-1860 (C)

Tin	Black(tons)	Stuff(tons)	Tin(tons)	Value(£)
1855	No detailed return			

Ownership: Comment 1862-1865 SUSPENDED

Management: Chief Agent 1859 Z.WILLIAMS & JAS.DONALD; 1860-1861
Z.WILLIAMS & F.KENT
Secretary 1859-1865 GEO.DOWN (P)

✳ DEVON BURRA BURRA TAVISTOCK SX 514742 0107 ✳

Production: Copper

	Ore(tons)	Metal(tons)	Value(£)
1863	156.00	7.40	520.00
1873	31.00	2.50	143.20

Comment 1863 (C) BURRA BURRA; 1873 (C) BURRA BURRA

DEVON BURRA BURRA   TAVISTOCK   Continued

Ownership: Comment 1860-1865 SUSPENDED
Management: Manager 1859 WM.CLEMO
            Chief Agent 1859 JOHN LORD
            Secretary 1859 W.A.PALMER (P)

DEVON CONSOLS   ASHBURTON   SX 666673 0108

Production: Tin No detailed return
Ownership: Comment 1863-1867 OR HUNTINGDON
Management: Chief Agent 1863-1867 M.DUNN
            Secretary 1863-1865 T.SPILLMAN; 1866-1867 JOHN BARROW

DEVON CONSOLS,EAST   BUCKFASTLEIGH   0109

Production: Copper No detailed return
Ownership: 1880-1883 EAST DEVON CONSOLS MINING CO.LTD.
            Comment 1883 NOT WORKING IN 1883
Management: Manager 1880-1881 JAS.BROWNING
            Chief Agent 1882-1883 JAS.BROWNING
            Secretary 1880-1881 EDW.CARTER
Employment: Underground   Surface   Total
            1880-1882   6   6

DEVON CONSOLS,EAST   TAVISTOCK   0110

Production: Copper No detailed return
Ownership: Comment 1864-1865 SUSPENDED
Management: Chief Agent 1859-1860 THOS.NEILL; 1861-1863 THOS.NEILL &
            THOS.RICHARDS
            Secretary 1859-1865 GEO.DOWN (P)

DEVON CONSOLS,NEW   LAMERTON   0111

Production: Lead   Ore(tons) Metal(tons)   Value(£)
            1870   14.50   10.80
            1871   No detailed return
Management: Chief Agent 1866 JOS.RICHARDS

DEVON COPPER   OKEHAMPTON   SX 565925 0112

Production: Copper No detailed return
Ownership: Comment 1865 SUSPENDED
Management: Chief Agent 1863-1864 THOS.NEILL
            Secretary 1863-1864 GEO.DOWN

38

DEVON COPPER AND BLENDE   LAMERTON   SX 433771 0113

Production: Zinc No detailed return
            Copper   Ore(tons) Metal(tons)   Value(£)
            1884   7.20   0.40   22.00
Ownership: 1880-1882 DEVON COPPER & BLENDE CO.LTD.
Management: Chief Agent 1880-1882 WM.B.SKEWIS
            Secretary 1880-1881 H.BAWDEN SKEWIS (S)
Employment: Underground   Surface   Total
            1880   12   20   32
            1881   21   31   52
            1882   6   6   12

DEVON COPPER,NEW   ASHBURTON   SX 744716 0114

Production: Copper No detailed return
Ownership: Comment 1863-1865 SUSPENDED
Management: Chief Agent 1860 PHIL.HAWKE; 1861-1862 PHIL.HAWKE & JOHN
            TREVARTHEN
            Secretary 1860 G.PAGE (P); 1861-1865 J.SPARKE AVERY (P)

DEVON FRANCES   BOVEY TRACEY   SX 783783 0115

Production: Copper No detailed return
Ownership: Comment 1866-1867 OR YARNER; 1868 SEE YARNER
Management: Chief Agent 1866-1867 W.WILLIAMS; 1869-1870 W.H.HOSKING;
            1871-1872 W.H.HOSKING & WM.GEORGE
            Secretary 1869-1870 H.BLANCHFORD (P); 1871 H.BLANCHFORD (S);
            1872 M.BAWDEN (P)

DEVON GREAT CONSOLS   TAVISTOCK   SX 426733 0116

Production: Copper   Ore(tons) Metal(tons)   Value(£)
            1848   16374.00   1684.10   93418.30
            1849   15777.00   1508.60   96934.70
            1850   17089.00   1632.30   109989.60
            1851   18921.00   1708.60   111082.00
            1852   20802.00   1659.10   134224.10
            1853   24120.00   1583.50   147281.30
            1854   23174.00   1486.10   143224.20
            1855   23467.00   1385.60   131294.10
            1856   29425.00   1687.10   143045.00
            1857   25746.00   1472.60   139770.40
            1858   23102.00   1352.10   116772.10
            1859   22832.00   1243.90   114033.70
            1860   21920.00   1224.50   109326.80
            1861   20801.00   1178.50   103072.50
            1862   24615.00   1448.10   116942.20
            1863   26756.00   1672.60   128799.10
            1864   25956.00   1613.30   136189.80
            1865   25259.00   1593.00   126932.30
            1866   22671.00   1453.50   98144.70

                                39

Copper	Ore(tons)	Metal(tons)	Value(£)
1867	20067.00	1333.30	94510.80
1868	20955.00	1391.50	92590.30
1869	16379.00	1010.40	62014.90
1870	16332.00	884.10	49729.70
1871	17413.00	868.80	50116.60
1872	15315.00	717.10	52942.20
1873	8716.00	428.50	24615.30
1874	5676.00	364.30	22920.60
1875	7085.00	416.50	29668.00
1876	9420.00	521.70	33626.10
1877	11383.60	613.40	34250.40
1878	9394.80	425.00	18307.20
1879	10261.00	518.80	22598.70
1880	10116.20	512.10	24929.90
1881	10922.70	442.10	20113.50
1882	11970.80	598.50	41897.00
1883	11127.20	459.00	20815.00
1884	10520.00		16827.00
1885	9778.00		11988.00
1886	6077.00		6498.00
1887	4209.00		6538.00
1888	4784.00		8501.00
1889	637.00		958.00
1890	4368.00		4310.00
1891	3142.00		3960.00
1892	2572.00		3475.00
1893	2312.00		3716.00
1894	2211.00		2907.00
1895	2008.00		3807.00
1896	1530.00		2971.00
1897	1417.00		2773.00
1898	1084.00	71.00	2188.00
1899	837.00		2224.00
1900	1015.00		2737.00
1901	842.00		1948.00
1902	268.00		370.00
1907	27.00		106.00

Comment 1848-1872 (C); 1873 (C) DEVON CONSOLS; 1874-1876 (C);
1907 OPEN WORKS

Tin	Black(tons)	Stuff(tons)	Tin(tons)	Value(£)
1886	2.10			115.00
1887-1888 No detailed return				
1892		65.00		170.00
1893	No detailed return			
1903	16.40			1223.00

Iron No detailed return

Arsenic	Ore(tons)	Metal(tons)	Value(£)
1868	473.50		2802.60
1869	1372.60		7726.70
1870	2237.10		12557.90
1871	2220.20		11863.00
1872	2222.30		11400.90

Arsenic	Ore(tons)	Metal(tons)	Value(£)
1873	1878.60		12100.50
1874	1842.00		12762.00
1875	1212.00		10503.10
1876	1521.60		14705.40
1877	2327.90		19029.50
1878	2481.80		16966.00
1879	3252.50		22848.30
1880	3148.80		26283.50
1881	2851.50		23325.00
1882	2760.10		22080.00
1883	2974.20		23793.00
1884	3198.30		25586.00
1885	3333.10		23588.00
1886	2428.20		18342.00
1887	2082.00		16659.00
1888	2100.00		19275.00
1889	2150.00		21137.00
1890	2615.00		28523.00
1891	2241.00		24406.00
1892	2174.00		20567.00
1893	3966.00		41372.00
1894	2212.00		24608.00
1895	1673.00		20268.00
1896	1521.00		20453.00
1897	1731.00		33835.00
1898	1723.00		24240.00
1899	1309.00		21669.00
1900	1408.00		25504.00
1901	1153.00		15000.70
1902	879.00		10513.00
1903	212.00		2403.00
1904	149.00		1406.00

Comment 1868 CRUDE ARSENIC; 1870 CRUDE ARSENIC; 1877 REFINED
ARSENIC A PORTION STOCKPILED; 1884-1886 REFINED ARSENIC

Arsenic Pyrite	Ore(tons)	Value(£)
1880	180.80	319.80
1906	277.00	520.00

Ownership: 1866-1873 THOS.MORRIS (P); 1876-1904 DEVON GREAT CONSOLS
CO.LTD.; 1906 DUKE OF BEDFORD; 1908 DUKE OF BEDFORD
Comment 1902 IN LIQUIDATION; 1903-1904 SUSPENDED
Management: Manager 1859-1862 JAS.RICHARDS; 1863-1865 THOS.MORRIS;
1866-1871 JAS.RICHARDS; 1872 IS.RICHARDS; 1873 JAS.RICHARDS;
1874-1876 IS.RICHARDS; 1877 JAS.RICHARDS; 1878 IS.RICHARDS;
1879-1881 G.F.RICHARDS
Chief Agent 1859 J.CLIMO; 1860-1862 WM.CLEMO; 1863-1865
JAS.RICHARDS & WM.CLEMO; 1866-1867 WM.CLEMO; 1868
WM.WOOLCOCK,WM.CLEMO & HY.GEORGE; 1869 HY.RODDA; 1870
WM.WOOLCOCK,WM.CLEMO & HY.GEORGE; 1871 HY.RODDA; 1872
WM.WOOLCOCK,WM.CLEMO & HY.GEORGE; 1873 HY.RODDA; 1874-1878
WM.CLEMO,HY.GEORGE & HY.RODDA; 1879 WM.WOOLCOCK; 1880
WM.CLEMO,HY.GEORGE & HY.RODDA; 1881 WM.WOOLCOCK; 1882-1890
IS.RICHARDS; 1892-1904 WM.CLEMO; 1906 E.C.RUNDLE; 1908

T.S.BLISS
Secretary 1859 J.MORRIS (P); 1860-1862 THOS.MORRIS (P);
1863-1871 ALEX.ALLEN (P); 1872-1880 ALEX.ALLEN (S); 1881
MOSES BAWDEN (P); 1891 GEO.HADLEE (S); 1892 MOSES BAWDEN (P);
1893 GEO.HADLEE (S); 1894 MOSES BAWDEN (P); 1895 GEO.HADLEE
(S); 1896 MOSES BAWDEN (P); 1897 GEO.HADLEE (S); 1898 MOSES
BAWDEN (P); 1899 GEO.HADLEE (S); 1900 MOSES BAWDEN (P); 1901
GEO.HADLEE (S); 1902 MOSES BAWDEN (P); 1903-1904 GEO.HADLEE
(S)

Employment:		Underground	Surface	Total
	1878	214	377	591
	1879	239	414	653
	1880	258	456	714
	1881	259	449	708
	1882	259	447	706
	1883	259	410	669
	1884	251	402	653
	1885	196	377	573
	1886	187	335	522
	1887	177	300	477
	1888	151	302	453
	1889	139	307	446
	1890	129	310	439
	1891	144	290	434
	1892	147	274	421
	1893	140	272	412
	1894	151	263	414
	1895	150	266	416
	1896	140	247	387
	1897	147	267	414
	1898	150	270	420
	1900	130	260	390
	1901	130	208	338
	1902	11	74	85
	1903		51	51
	1904		13	13
	1906		6	6
	1908		26	26

DEVON GREAT ELIZABETH   ASHBURTON   SX 710707 0117

Production: Copper No detailed return
Ownership: Comment 1860-1865 SUSPENDED
Management: Manager 1859 WM.GOYEN

DEVON GREAT ELLEN   ASHBURTON   0118

Production: Copper No detailed return
            Tin No detailed return
Ownership: Comment 1864-1865 SUSPENDED
Management: Chief Agent 1860-1863 WM.TAYLOR

DEVON GREAT ELLEN   ASHBURTON   Continued

    Secretary 1861-1865 THOS.SHOWELL (P)

DEVON GREAT MARIA   LAMERTON   SX 395738 0119

Production: Copper No detailed return
Management: Manager 1866 JOS.RICHARDS

DEVON GREAT UNITED   LAMERTON   SX 413740 0120

Production: Copper   Ore(tons) Metal(tons)   Value(£)
            1883   94.80   4.70   181.00
            1884   460.00   1436.00
            1888   43.00   220.00
            1889   50.00   128.00
            1890   456.00   1661.00
            1891   276.00   975.00
            1892   77.00   233.00
            Comment 1888-1892 DEVON UNITED
            Arsenic Pyrite Ore(tons)   Value(£)
            1888   29.00   18.00
            1890   65.00   90.00
            1891   110.00   134.00
            1892   51.00   36.00
            Comment 1888-1892 DEVON UNITED
Ownership: 1880-1884 DEVON GREAT UNITED MINING CO.LTD.; 1888-1891 DEVON
            UNITED CO.LTD.
            Comment 1891 ABANDONED
Management: Chief Agent 1880-1884 IS.RICHARDS; 1888-1890 IS.RICHARDS
            Secretary 1880-1881 MOSES BAWDEN; 1888-1890 MOSES BAWDEN;
            1891 GEO.HADLEE & MOSES BAWDEN
Employment: Underground   Surface   Total
            1880   12   14   26
            1881   19   23   42
            1882   26   18   44
            1883   25   12   37
            1884   27   13   40
            1888   18   18   36
            1889   18   8   26
            1890   23   10   33
            1891   20   13   33
            1892   4   2   6

DEVON KAPUNDA   SYDENHAM DAMEREL   SX 403754 0121

Management: Manager 1859 JOS.COCK
            Chief Agent 1859 WM.COCK
            Secretary 1859 T.NICHOLLS (P)

DEVON POLDICE   BUCKLAND MONACHORUM   SX 493707 0122

Production:
Copper	Ore(tons)	Metal(tons)	Value(£)	
1867	46.00	2.50	167.90	

Comment 1867 (C)

Tin	Black(tons)	Stuff(tons)	Tin(tons)	Value(£)
1862	11.80			795.10
1873	0.80			52.70
1875	5.60			266.50

Comment 1873 POLDICE
Ownership: Comment 1872-1873 POLDICE
Management: Manager 1872-1875 R.LEGASSICK
Chief Agent 1859-1866 JOHN LEAN; 1875 JAS.MURRAY
Secretary 1859-1866 JOHN LEAN (P)

DEVON TIN   DARTMEET   SX 668738 0123

Production:
Tin	Black(tons)	Stuff(tons)	Tin(tons)	Value(£)
1855	1.10			48.00

DEVON UNION   MARYTAVY   SX 505766 0124

Production: Copper No detailed return
Ownership: Comment 1863-1865 SUSPENDED
Management: Manager 1860-1862 Z.WILLIAMS
Chief Agent 1859 Z.WILLIAMS & JAS.DONALD; 1860-1862
JAS.DONALD
Secretary 1859-1860 WM.WATSON (P); 1861-1865 E.S.CODD (P)

DEVON UNITED   PETER TAVY   SX 512786 0125

Production:
Copper	Ore(tons)	Metal(tons)	Value(£)	
1905	19.00		48.00	
1906	207.00		840.00	

Tin	Black(tons)	Stuff(tons)	Tin(tons)	Value(£)
1852	10.90			
1905	4.40	187.00		925.00
1906	21.30			2275.00
1907	28.80			3004.00
1908	45.40			3537.00
1909	50.80			4310.00
1910	53.00			4936.00
1911	47.00			5500.00
1912	71.00			9500.00
1913	54.00			6895.00

Comment 1852 POSSIBLY NOT SAME MINE; 1905 TIN STUFF EST.

Arsenic	Ore(tons)	Metal(tons)	Value(£)
1907	41.00		810.00
1908	148.00		1615.00
1909	107.00		829.00
1910	143.00		869.00
1911	205.00		1026.00

Arsenic	Ore(tons)	Metal(tons)	Value(£)
1912	231.00		1950.00
1913	119.00		975.00

Arsenic Pyrite	Ore(tons)	Value(£)
1905	94.00	134.00

Comment 1905 ORE EST

Ownership: 1901-1912 DEVON UNITED MINES SYNDICATE LTD.; 1913 DEVON UNITED MINES (1906) LTD.

Management: Chief Agent 1901-1902 W.J.BOWHAY; 1910-1913 G.M.LADDS

Employment:

	Underground	Surface	Total
1901	10	3	13
1902	2	1	3
1903	10	10	20
1904	8	9	17
1905	9	9	18
1906	23	18	41
1907	35	33	68
1908	25	32	57
1909	25	41	66
1910	41	32	73
1911	44	43	87
1912	43	40	83
1913	39	47	86

DEVON UNITED,SOUTH   BUCKFASTLEIGH   SX 718675 0126

Production:

Copper	Ore(tons)	Metal(tons)	Value(£)
1880	1079.90	59.40	2755.40
1881	2157.00	122.90	6428.70
1882	1906.80	109.60	6673.00
1883	1744.80	69.40	3490.00
1884	1174.00		2296.00
1885	126.00		217.00

Arsenic Pyrite	Ore(tons)	Value(£)
1883	84.00	72.00

Ownership: 1879-1887 SOUTH DEVON UNITED COPPER MINING CO.
Comment 1880-1881 FORMERLY BROOKWOOD & EMMA; 1885-1887 NOT WORKED

Management: Manager 1880-1881 WM.HOOPER
Chief Agent 1880 WM.HOOPER; 1881-1882 PHIL.RICHARDSON & J.CHIGWIDEN; 1883-1887 WM.HOOPER
Secretary 1880-1881 MOSES BAWDEN (P)

Employment:

	Underground	Surface	Total
1878		5	5
1879	12	11	23
1880	50	43	93
1881	77	46	123
1882	79	41	120
1883	54	37	91
1884	40	19	59

Production: Lead & Silver   Ore(tons) Lead(tons) Silver(ozs)   Value(£)

	Ore(tons)	Lead(tons)	Silver(ozs)	Value(£)
1863	20.40	14.10		
1864	141.00	91.60	270.00	
1865	250.10	162.50	486.00	
1866	44.20	34.00	252.00	

Ownership: Comment 1866 NORTH DEVON CONSOLS
Management: Chief Agent 1860-1865 JOHN BLAMEY & J.COCK; 1866 JOHN BLAMEY
            Secretary 1866 THOS.FIDLER

Production: Iron   Ore(tons)   Iron(%)   Value(£)

	Ore(tons)	Iron(%)	Value(£)
1859	No detailed return		
1872	380.00		228.00
1873	476.50		450.00
1874	255.00		191.20

            Comment 1859 SEE PORTLEMOUTH CONSOLS; 1872-1874 HE.
            Umber No detailed return
Ownership: 1870-1876 VAN IRON ORE CO.; 1878 BEER,MUSGRAVE & CO.
Management: Chief Agent 1870-1876 W.H.HOSKING; 1878 NICH.PASCOE

✳ ✳

Production: Manganese   Ore(tons) Metal(tons)   Value(£)

	Ore(tons)	Metal(tons)	Value(£)
1874	40.00		200.00
1875	37.00		185.00

Ownership: 1880-1883 DEVON MANGANESE MINING CO.LTD.
            Comment 1880-1881 DEVON MANGANESE; 1882 DEVON MANGANESE NOT
            WORKED; 1883 DEVON MANGANESE
Management: Chief Agent 1873-1874 THOS.GREGORY; 1875 WM.HOOPER; 1880-1881
            GEO.SEYMOUR
            Secretary 1873-1874 JOHN LOMAS & CO.; 1875 SCHOLEFIELD &
            LOMAS; 1881-1883 JAS.BEAZLEY (S)
Employment: Underground   Surface   Total

	Underground	Surface	Total
1880	14	14	28
1881	2	12	14

Production: Iron   Ore(tons)   Iron(%)   Value(£)

	Ore(tons)	Iron(%)	Value(£)
1858	54.50		29.90

            1859-1861 No detailed return
            Comment 1858 BH.; 1859 BH.SEE PORTLEMOUTH CONSOLS; 1860-1861
            BH.
Ownership: Comment 1863-1865 SUSPENDED

★ DIPPERTOWN   MARYSTOWE   SX 423853 0132 ★

Production: Manganese No detailed return
Management: Manager 1860-1867 JOHN SIMS
            Chief Agent 1860-1867 N.TRUSCOTT
            Secretary 1860-1867 JOHN SIMS (P)

DODDISCOMBELEIGH   DODDISCOMBSLEIGH   SX 844863 0133

Production: Manganese No detailed return
Management: Chief Agent 1875 JAS.DUNSMORE

DOWN,WEST   WEST DOWN   0134

Production: Iron No detailed return
Ownership: 1876 A.N.HIGGINS
Management: Chief Agent 1876 A.N.HIGGINS

★ DOWN,WEST   WHITCHURCH   SX 488705 0135 ★

Management: Chief Agent 1864-1865 THOS.NEILL
            Secretary 1864-1865 GEO.DOWN

DRAKEWALLS   CALSTOCK, CORNWALL   SX 424707 0136

Ownership: 1900 DRAKEWALLS CO.LTD.
Management: Secretary 1900 JOHN TAYLOR & SON

DREWS   BRIXHAM   0137

Production: Iron   Ore(tons)   Iron(%)   Value(£)
            1866   15175.00   5320.50
            1867   No detailed return
            Comment 1866 BH.VALUE INC.CHINTER &SHARKHAM; 1867 1866VALUE
            INC.FURGAM HILL ALSO
Ownership: 1866 WM.BROWNE
Management: Chief Agent 1866 PHAR.GROSE

DRUID   BUCKFASTLEIGH   SX 744716 0138

Production: Copper   Ore(tons) Metal(tons)   Value(£)
            1867   14.00   0.40   25.50
            1868   24.00   0.90   49.80
            Comment 1867 (C) DRUIDS; 1868 (C)
Ownership: Comment 1866-1867 FORMERLY THE ARUNDEL MINES; 1868-1869
            FORMERLY ARUNDEL BECOMING VICTORIA; 1870 FORMERLY ARUNDEL NOW
            THE VICTORIA
Management: Manager 1868 STEP.PAUL; 1869-1870 WM.SKEWIS
            Chief Agent 1866 CAPT.WILLIAMS & STEP.PAUL; 1867 STEP.PAUL;

47

1869 MOSES BAWDEN & WM.GEORGE; 1870 WM.GEORGE
Secretary 1869 H.BARTON; 1870 MOSES BAWDEN

✳ DUKE,LITTLE   TAVISTOCK   SX 471695 0139 ✳

Production: Arsenic No detailed return
            Arsenic Pyrite   Ore(tons)   Value(£)
            1907   119.00   361.00
            1908   47.00   91.00
Ownership: 1907-1913 DUKE OF BEDFORD
Management: Chief Agent 1907-1913 T.S.BLISS
Employment: Underground   Surface   Total
            1907   1   1   2
            1908   2   2

✳ EDGECUMBE   MILTON ABBOT   SX 397791 0140 ✳

Production: Manganese   Ore(tons) Metal(tons)   Value(£)
            1874   20.00   80.00
            1876   10.00   45.00
            Umber No detailed return
Ownership: 1875-1876 EDGECUMBE MINING CO.; 1880 THOS.NEILL & OTHERS;
            1881 EDGECUMBE MANGANESE MINING CO.LTD.
            Comment 1860-1865 EDGECOMBE SEE CLINTON; 1881 NOT WORKED
Management: Chief Agent 1874 JOS.BATE; 1875-1876 R.WALTERS; 1880-1881
            THOS.NEILL
            Secretary 1873-1874 JAS.MURRAY; 1880-1881 E.C.WRIGHT (S)
Employment: Underground   Surface   Total
            1880   6   6

ELEANOR,GREAT   NORTH BOVEY   SX 735833 0141

Production: Tin   Black(tons) Stuff(tons) Tin(tons)   Value(£)
            1876   3.00   129.00
            1877   0.90   36.60
            1878   10.80   326.10
            1879   1.00   55.00
            1880   3.00   136.50
Ownership: 1876 GREAT WHEAL ELEANOR CO.; 1877-1883 GREAT WHEAL ELEANOR
            TIN MINING CO.LTD.
Management: Manager 1879 W.H.HOSKING
            Chief Agent 1876 JOHN TREDINNICK; 1877 W.H.HOSKING; 1878
            W.H.HOSKING & JAS.PAGE; 1880 JOHN TREDINNICK; 1881-1883
            W.H.HOSKING
Employment: Underground   Surface   Total
            1878   6   3   9
            1879   4   4
            1880   9   6   15
            1881   4   1   5
            1882   2   2

	Underground	Surface	Total
1883		2	2

✳ EMILY   OKEHAMPTON   SX 650930 0142 ✳

Production: Copper

	Ore(tons)	Metal(tons)	Value(£)
1859	169.00	6.80	596.60
1877	273.50	14.30	698.00
1878	59.00	6.30	364.20
1878	71.00	7.50	391.90
1878	130.00	13.80	756.10
1879	41.60	2.00	105.70
1879	96.60	4.80	245.50
1879	55.00	2.80	139.80
1882	110.00	4.40	165.00
1883	172.90	15.50	595.00
1885	220.00		847.00
1886	430.00		1570.00
1887	85.00		197.00
1889	40.00		100.00

Comment 1877 LATE FURSDON; 1878 (I); 1878 (S); 1878 1878
TOTAL; 1879 (S); 1879 (I); 1879 1879 TOTAL; 1882 UNDRESSED
ORE

Ownership: 1877-1892 EMILY MINING CO.
Comment 1876 SEE FURSDON; 1877-1879 EMILY LATE FURSDON;
1880-1881 EMILY LATE FURSDON NOT WORKED; 1890-1891 NOW
ABANDONED; 1892 SUSPENDED THROUGHOUT 1892; 1899-1911 SEE
RAMSLEY

Management: Manager 1877 M.ERN.JOBLING
Chief Agent 1878-1881 JOHN CROCKER; 1887-1892 D.S.WARNE
Secretary 1877 WM.BATTYE; 1878-1885 M.ERN.JOBLING; 1886
D.S.WARNE

Employment:

	Underground	Surface	Total
1878	6	6	12
1879	6	4	10
1880	3		3
1882	40	41	81
1883	20	10	30
1884	2		2
1885	24	16	40
1886	16	12	28
1887	9		9
1888	2	1	3
1889	8	2	10
1892		1	1

EMMA   BUCKFASTLEIGH   SX 715675 0143

Production: Copper

	Ore(tons)	Metal(tons)	Value(£)
1856	65.00	6.20	549.20
1856	370.00	26.00	2507.70

Copper	Ore(tons)	Metal(tons)	Value(£)
1856	305.00	19.80	1958.50
1857	745.00	57.40	5720.30
1858	533.00	32.40	2921.80
1859	737.00	41.40	3654.80
1859	586.00	30.50	2550.80
1859	151.00	10.90	1104.00
1860	1546.00	90.70	7897.70
1861	1849.00	84.60	6903.50
1862	1686.00	98.10	7812.70
1863	1533.00	70.60	5052.40
1864	859.00	34.50	2779.40
1865	986.00	35.30	2580.90
1866	787.00	64.90	4581.20
1867	823.00	58.30	4206.00
1868	366.00	19.60	1342.00
1875	223.00	13.80	1043.20
1876	304.00	13.40	845.80
1877	108.00	5.10	293.00

Comment 1856 (S); 1856 1856 TOTAL; 1856 (C); 1857–1859 (C); 1859 (S); 1859 1859 TOTAL; 1860–1868 (C); 1875–1876 (C)
Ownership: 1876–1877 WHEAL EMMA TIN & COPPER MINE CO.LTD.; 1878–1879 SOUTH DEVON UNITED MINING CO.
Comment 1880–1881 SEE SOUTH DEVON UNITED
Management: Manager 1859 WM.EDWARDS; 1874 WM.HARRIS
Chief Agent 1859 ? BARRETT; 1860–1862 ROBT.DUNSTAN; 1863–1866 J.BENNETT; 1867 I.BENNETT; 1868–1872 THOS.BENNETT; 1873 SAMP.KEAST; 1875 SAMP.KEAST; 1876–1879 WM.HOOPER & SAMP.KEAST
Secretary 1860 H.CODD (P); 1861–1872 E.S.CODD; 1873–1878 WM.BATTYE

EMMENS UNITED MINES   CALLINGTON, CORNWALL   SX 359719 0144

Production: Copper   Ore(tons) Metal(tons)   Value(£)
1874   2000.00   24.00
Comment 1874 (P) INC.NEW CONSOLS

EX   0145

Production: Lead   Ore(tons) Metal(tons)   Value(£)
1851   18.00   13.00
1852–1853 No detailed return

EXMOOR   DULVERTON, SOMERSET   SS 797378 0146

Ownership: 1909 EXMOOR MINING SYNDICATE

Production: Lead & Silver

	Ore(tons)	Lead(tons)	Silver(ozs)	Value(£)
1851	230.00	141.90		
1852	634.60	443.70	2500.00	
1853	726.00	472.00	5980.00	
1854	1140.00	800.00	15000.00	
1855	1285.00	810.00	18630.00	
1856	1447.00	955.00	19100.00	
1857	1288.00	745.00	23090.00	
1858	1345.00	793.00	18328.00	
1859	1345.00	887.00	16853.00	
1860	629.90	415.10	7895.00	
1861	553.00	347.00	3817.00	
1862	130.00	80.00	1130.00	
1865	144.10	93.60	466.00	
1866	No detailed return			
1867	119.50	83.30	966.00	
1870	50.90	37.50	165.00	
1871	67.50	46.90	188.00	
1872	88.60	61.60	242.00	
1873	223.00	156.10	624.00	2631.50
1874	86.10	61.60	246.00	

Comment 1854-1857 INC.ADAMS

Zinc

	Ore(tons)	Metal(tons)	Value(£)
1859	164.00		514.30
1860	40.90		121.70
1863	49.00		147.00
1870	346.20		970.30
1871	570.60		1562.50
1872	266.40		1607.70
1873	123.50		741.00

Comment 1863 EXMOUTH ETC.; 1873 EXMOUTH SILVER LEAD MINES

Copper No detailed return

Ownership: Comment 1862-1863 SUSPENDED; 1873 STOPPED 1873

Management: Manager 1859 WM.SKEWIS; 1871-1872 JOHN COCK; 1873 JOHN
NICHOLLS
Chief Agent 1859 JOHN NICHOLLS; 1860 J.P.NICHOLLS; 1861
F.P.NICHOLLS; 1865-1867 JAS.HAMPTON & N.FAULL; 1868
RICH.TREVITHICK & J.FAULL; 1869 JAS.HAMPTON & J.FAULL; 1870
JOHN COCK & J.FAULL; 1871-1872 J.FAULL; 1873-1875 JOHN COCK
Secretary 1859-1863 C.WESTCOMBE; 1864-1867 H.E.CROKER;
1869-1875 RICH.TREVITHICK

EXMOUTH,NORTH   CHRISTOW   SX 836837 0148

Production: Lead

	Ore(tons)	Metal(tons)	Value(£)
1860	16.50	11.20	
1861	No detailed return		

Zinc

	Ore(tons)	Metal(tons)	Value(£)
1860	73.00		219.00

Copper No detailed return

Ownership: Comment 1860-1861 FORMERLY AMERY & ADAMS; 1862-1865 FORMERLY
AMERY & ADAMS SUSPENDED

EXMOUTH,NORTH   CHRISTOW   Continued

Management: Manager 1860-1861 WM.SKEWIS
            Chief Agent 1860 HY.HARVEY; 1861 W.JOURY
            Secretary 1860-1865 G.LAVINGTON (P)

EXMOUTH,SOUTH   HENNOCK   SX 835807 0149

Production: Lead & Silver   Ore(tons)   Lead(tons) Silver(ozs)   Value(£)
            1862   486.00   350.00   1800.00
            1863   281.80   202.30   1010.00
            1864   52.00   33.80   168.00
            1865   18.10   12.00   60.00
            1866   7.80   5.80   28.00
            1867   21.00   12.00   90.00
            Iron No detailed return
Ownership: 1872 C.C.IRON MINES CO.LTD.
Management: Manager 1860-1867 J.P.NICHOLLS; 1873-1875 HY.RICKARD
            Chief Agent 1860 T.MEDLIN; 1861 J.NEAL; 1862-1864 J.MAUNDER;
            1865-1867 G.MAUNDER; 1872 JOHN CORNISH
            Secretary 1860-1866 C.WESTCOMBE; 1867 J.O.HARRIS; 1873-1875
            S.O.HARRIS

✳ FERNHILL   LIFTON   SX 360870 0150 ✳

Ownership: 1894-1895 FERNHILL GOLD REEFS SYNDICATE LTD.
            Comment 1894-1895 WORK NOT ACTUALLY COMMENCED
Management: Secretary 1894-1895 H.CLENCH SENR.

FIVE ACRES   BRIXHAM   0151

Production: Iron   Ore(tons)   Iron(%)   Value(£)
            1865   No detailed return
            1868   3988.30   1196.40
            1872   No detailed return
            Comment 1865 BH.SEE SHARKHAM; 1868 BH.; 1872 BH.SEE TORBAY
            IRON
Ownership: 1865-1871 WM.BROWNE
            Comment 1872-1874 SEE TORBAY IRON
Management: Chief Agent 1865-1871 PHAR.GROSE

✳ FLORENCE   LYDFORD   SX 514847 0152 ✳

Production: Lead   Ore(tons) Metal(tons)   Value(£)
            1858   6.00   4.00
            1859-1860 No detailed return

                                  52

Production: Lead

	Ore(tons)	Metal(tons)	Value(£)
1884	2.00	1.00	12.00
1885	3.00	1.00	18.00
1886	20.00	7.00	130.00

Copper

	Ore(tons)	Metal(tons)	Value(£)
1884	5.00		25.00
1885	5.00		29.00
1886	30.00		150.00

Iron

	Ore(tons)	Iron(%)	Value(£)
1873	3000.00		2250.00
1874	4386.00		3125.00
1875	1215.00		911.00
1876	5712.00		2856.00
1877	3611.00		1805.50
1878	2769.00		1384.50
1880	5593.00		5593.00
1881	5300.00		3842.00
1882	5000.00	52.50	3625.00
1883	1500.00		1087.00
1885	300.00		120.00

            Comment 1873-1878 SP.FLORENCE; 1880-1883 RH.; 1885 BH.
Ownership: 1873-1879 FLORENCE MINING CO.LTD.; 1880-1892 NEW FLORENCE
            MINING CO.LTD.; 1893 NEW FLORENCE MINES SYNDICATE
            Comment 1873-1878 FLORENCE; 1879 FLORENCE NOT WORKED;
            1880-1881 FLORENCE; 1887 NOT WORKING; 1888-1889 SUSPENDED;
            1890-1891 IN LIQUIDATION; 1892 SUSPENDED THROUGHOUT 1892
Management: Manager 1873 GEO.BUSH; 1875-1881 DUD.J.C.BUSH
            Chief Agent 1874 SID.HAWKINS; 1891-1893 DUD.J.C.BUSH
            Secretary 1882-1890 DUD.J.C.BUSH
Employment:

	Underground	Surface	Total
1878	21	8	29
1880	51	12	63
1881	24	13	37
1882	32	14	46
1883	10	14	24
1884	10	7	17
1885	13	5	18
1886	7	3	10
1888		2	2
1889		1	1
1891	2		2
1892-1893		1	1

Production: Arsenic No detailed return
Ownership: 1897-1903 SIR HY.HOARE
            Comment 1903 SUSPENDED
Management: Chief Agent 1898-1903 W.H.HOSKING
Employment:

	Underground	Surface	Total
1897-1898	4		4
1900-1902	2		2

✳ FOREST   OKEHAMPTON   SX 561912 0155 ✳

Production: Lead No detailed return
            Tin No detailed return
Management: Secretary 1869-1870 THOS.WATTS (P)

✳ FORTESCUE   LAMERTON   SX 414739 0156 ✳

Production: Lead & Silver   Ore(tons) Lead(tons) Silver(ozs)   Value(£)
            1855   22.00   12.00   2640.00
            1873   No detailed return
            Comment 1873 SEE WEST MARIA
            Copper   Ore(tons) Metal(tons)   Value(£)
            1866-1878 No detailed return
            Comment 1866-1870 SEE MARIA; 1871-1875 SEE WEST MARIA;
            1876-1878 SEE MARIA
            Tin   Black(tons) Stuff(tons)   Tin(tons)   Value(£)
            1873-1874 No detailed return
            Comment 1873-1874 SEE WEST MARIA
Ownership: Comment 1860-1879 SEE WEST MARIA
Employment: Underground   Surface   Total
            1878
            Comment 1878 WEST FORTESCUE.SEE MARIA

FORTUNE   0157

Production: Copper   Ore(tons) Metal(tons)   Value(£)
            1860   216.00   55.40   5514.70
            Comment 1860 (S)

FOWSHAM   BRIXHAM   0158

Production: Iron No detailed return
Ownership: 1866 BEN.SMITH
Management: Chief Agent 1866 JNO.BROKENSHIRE

✳ FRANCO   HORRABRIDGE   SX 508702 0159 ✳

Production: Copper   Ore(tons) Metal(tons)   Value(£)
            1852   244.00   12.80   1090.20
            1853   500.00   21.50   1958.30
            1854   727.00   24.30   2140.70
            1855   487.00   19.40   1813.40
            1856   209.00   13.30   1248.20
            1857   118.00   6.20   609.50
            1858   450.00   21.40   1891.00
            1859   369.00   15.30   1410.10
            1860   319.00   15.30   1386.00
            1861   243.00   14.00   1236.20
            1870   28.00   1.30   72.80
            1871   100.00   3.60   202.10

                                      54

Copper	Ore(tons)	Metal(tons)	Value(£)
1872	18.00	2.00	176.60
1873	45.00	2.80	163.10

Comment 1852-1861 (C); 1870-1873 (C) FRANCO CONSOLS
Tin No detailed return
Ownership: Comment 1862-1865 SUSPENDED; 1870-1875 FRANCO CONSOLS
Management: Manager 1859-1861 JOHN LEAN
            Chief Agent 1870-1875 WM.DOIDGE
            Secretary 1859-1865 C.V.BRIDGEMAN (P); 1869-1875 WM.NEWTON

FRANKMILLS   CHRISTOW   SX 836820 0160

Production: Lead & Silver	Ore(tons)	Lead(tons)	Silver(ozs)	Value(£)
1857	311.70	197.00	1379.00	
1858	547.00	350.00	1890.00	
1859	737.00	471.40	3014.00	
1860	767.60	490.80	2945.00	
1861	961.20	615.00	3690.00	
1862	630.00	396.00	11830.00	
1863	726.00	479.00	8666.00	
1864	1209.00	785.80	17682.00	
1865	1337.90	815.00	31785.00	
1866	451.90	275.70	10750.00	
1867	428.80	256.00	9984.00	
1868	1519.80	1139.00	39865.00	
1869	1057.80	659.70	27437.00	
1870	957.10	622.00	23925.00	
1871	761.00	532.70	13300.00	
1872	565.00	395.50	9887.00	
1873	293.00	205.10	5125.00	3557.50
1874	237.10	165.90	5925.00	3252.30
1875	250.00	187.50	3740.00	
1876	376.30	282.20	5640.00	4070.80
1877	332.70	249.30	4900.00	2702.80
1878	219.80	160.00	3246.00	2628.00
1879	119.90	90.00	1825.00	1440.00
1880	15.00	10.80	100.00	42.00

Comment 1869   TWO RETURNS AGGREGATED; 1880 SOLD.IN
LIQUIDATION

Barytes	Ore(tons)	Value(£)
1876	6.50	
1877	867.10	325.20

Iron	Ore(tons)	Iron(%)	Value(£)
1872	20.00		13.00
1874	70.00		105.00
1875	100.00		55.00
1877	12.00		8.40
1879	30.00		15.00
1880	190.00		95.00

Comment 1872 BH.; 1874 BH.; 1875 SP.; 1877 SP.; 1879-1880
BH.

Fluorspar	Ore(tons)	Value(£)
1880	176.00	88.00

Ownership: 1875–1881 FRANKMILLS MINING CO.
Comment 1878–1879 WINDING UP IN STANNARY COURT
Management: Manager 1859 J.P.NICHOLLS; 1868–1872 JNO.CORNISH; 1873
S.T.NICHOLLS; 1874–1875 JOHN NICHOLLS
Chief Agent 1860–1861 JAS.HAMPTON; 1862–1863 J.P.NICHOLLS &
JNO.CORNISH; 1864 J.P.NICHOLLS,JNO.CORNISH & R.ANDREW; 1865
J.P.NICHOLLS,JNO.CORNISH & P.CORNISH; 1866–1867
J.P.NICHOLLS,JNO.CORNISH & F.CORNISH; 1868–1869 F.CORNISH;
1870–1872 F.CORNISH & N.ADAMS; 1873 JAS.ROWE & N.ADAMS;
1874–1875 JAS.ROWE JUN. & N.ADAMS; 1876–1877
RICH.SOUTHEY,JAS.ROWE JUN. & N.ADAMS; 1878 JAS.ROWE &
N.ADAMS; 1879–1881 W.T.BRYANT & N.ADAMS
Secretary 1859–1866 C.WESTCOMBE (P); 1867–1881 J.O.HARRIS

Employment:
	Underground	Surface	Total
1878	32	63	95
1879	8	47	55
1880		21	21

FREDERICK   LYDFORD   0161

Ownership: Comment 1862–1865 SUSPENDED
Management: Manager 1860–1861 W.E.CUMMINS
Chief Agent 1860–1861 C.BARTLE
Secretary 1860–1865 W.E.CUMMINS (P)

FRIENDSHIP   MARYTAVY   SX 508794 0162

Production:
Lead & Silver	Ore(tons)	Lead(tons)	Silver(ozs)	Value(£)
1848	9.00	5.00		
1849	5.00	3.00		
1850	No detailed return			
1851	3.10	2.10		
1852	10.00	7.00		
1853	No detailed return			
1854	17.90	12.50	112.00	
1858	5.20	3.10		
1859	No detailed return			
1860	1.70	1.00		
1861	2.00	1.30		
1865	2.30	1.60		
1866	No detailed return			
1868	2.70	2.00		
1869	2.70	2.00		
1870	4.10	3.00		
1871	5.70	3.90	20.00	
1872	4.80	3.50	17.00	
1874	3.40	2.60	10.00	49.90
1875	2.90	2.20		40.40

Zinc	Ore(tons)	Metal(tons)	Value(£)
1858	160.00		440.50

Copper	Ore(tons)	Metal(tons)	Value(£)
1849	2484.00	275.90	18988.60
1850	2490.00	258.10	18673.60
1851	2474.00	238.20	16408.50
1853	1733.00	165.70	16913.40
1855	1809.00	161.10	17067.20
1856	1637.00	146.60	14037.40
1857	1699.00	154.00	15748.50
1858	1510.00	144.70	13686.40
1859	1674.00	154.50	14943.70
1860	1676.00	167.90	15835.10
1861	1661.00	143.50	12885.70
1862	1767.00	155.00	12932.30
1863	1532.00	133.70	10652.70
1864	1594.00	138.30	12053.40
1865	1941.00	169.50	13814.80
1866	2017.00	181.60	12703.90
1867	1612.00	121.20	8646.00
1868	1048.00	71.00	4777.90
1870	1090.00	97.40	5982.00
1871	1167.00	100.80	6264.20
1872	926.00	63.80	5053.00
1873	287.00	21.90	1287.60
1874	156.00	14.80	1017.60
1875	160.00	14.40	1107.00
1876	92.00	9.10	617.70
1877	20.10	1.40	104.80
1880	21.90	3.70	75.00
1882	47.00	2.80	236.00
1883	65.00	4.20	390.00
1884	21.00		83.00

Comment 1849-1851 (C); 1853 (C); 1855-1868 (C); 1870-1876 (C); 1882-1884 DEVON FRIENDSHIP

Tin	Black(tons)	Stuff(tons)	Tin(tons)	Value(£)
1877	3.50			64.50
1878	26.70			743.80
1879	18.50			585.10
1880	20.60			825.40
1881	10.30		6.80	529.00
1882	10.50		6.30	499.00
1883	13.20			582.00
1884	10.70			448.00
1909	2.00			114.00
1910	1.40			119.00
1913	17.60			1954.00

Comment 1882-1884 DEVON FRIENDSHIP; 1913 INC.JEWEL

Arsenic	Ore(tons)	Metal(tons)	Value(£)
1858	160.00		120.00
1861	671.90		240.90
1874	382.70		458.70
1875	660.40		5339.60

Arsenic	Ore(tons)	Metal(tons)	Value(£)
1877	599.00		4792.00
1878	370.60		1448.30
1879	574.30		3018.30
1880	545.90		3182.90
1881	530.00		2511.70
1882	440.00		2313.00
1883	419.00		2399.00
1884	515.00		3090.00
1891	60.00		438.00
1897	230.00		4535.00
1898	278.00		4323.00
1900	208.00		3600.00
1909	711.00		8532.00
1910	184.00		2021.00
1912	24.00		144.00

Comment 1858 ARSENICAL PYRITES; 1861 CRUDE ARSENIC; 1882-1884
DEVON FRIENDSHIP; 1913 SEE WHEAL JEWEL

Tungsten	Ore(tons)	Metal(tons)	Value(£)
1909	1.00		45.00

Arsenic Pyrite	Ore(tons)	Value(£)
1875	844.60	1108.00
1876	4000.00	3600.00
1878	3.00	15.50
1892	40.00	37.00
1893	135.00	135.00
1894	268.00	301.00
1896	1200.00	1500.00
1899	3047.00	3047.00
1908	1655.00	1837.00

Comment 1876 ARSENICAL MUNDIC VALUE EST; 1896 LANYONS SHAFT &
WHEAL FRIENDSHIP
Ownership: 1878-1879 ALF.LANYON; 1880-1885 DEVON FRIENDSHIP MINING CO.;
1891 MR.BOWHAY; 1892-1894 HY.PEARCE; 1895-1900 DEVON ARSENIC
MANUFACTURING CO.LTD.; 1907-1909 E.H.BAYLDON; 1910-1911 WHEAL
JEWELL SYNDICATE LTD.; 1912-1913 WHEAL JEWELL & MARY TAVY
MINES LTD.
Comment 1873 DRESSING MUNDIC ONLY; 1880-1885 DEVON
FRIENDSHIP; 1892 DRESSING WASTE HEAPS; 1893 BENNETTS SHAFT;
1896-1900 FRIENDSHIP & LANYONS SHAFT; 1911 SUSPENDED;
1912-1913 REOPENED APR.1912
Management: Manager 1859 Z.WILLIAMS; 1860-1868 JOS.MATTHEWS; 1869-1871
Z.WILLIAMS; 1875 J.C.LANYON & SONS; 1876-1879 ALF.LANYON;
1880-1881 JOHN DAW; 1913 MURRAY
Chief Agent 1860-1868 Z.WILLIAMS; 1869-1871 F.KENT; 1872
F.KENT & MICH.MORCOM; 1873 MICH.MORCOM; 1874 JOHN JAMES &
JOHN LEAN; 1875 JOHN JAMES & JAS.TREDINNICK; 1876-1880
JAS.TREDINNICK; 1881 JAS.TREDINNICK & WM.GILL; 1882-1884
F.R.W.DAW; 1892-1894 W.J.BOWHAY; 1895-1897 WM.GILL; 1898-1899
W.J.BOWHAY; 1900 RICH.DUNSTAN; 1910-1913 ERN.TERRELL
Secretary 1859 JOS.MATTHEWS (P); 1860-1872 JOHN TAYLOR&SONS
(P); 1873-1874 J.C.LANYON; 1875-1876 JAS.JENKIN; 1877
JAS.JENKIN (P); 1878-1879 JAS.JENKIN; 1880-1881 J.H.A.SMITH

(S); 1885 JNO.PEARCE; 1895-1900 J.L.PEARCE; 1907-1909
D.H.BAYLDON; 1913 BROWNING & FLEMING

Employment:	Underground	Surface	Total
1878	4	67	71
1879	13	75	88
1880	18	82	100
1881	36	93	129
1882	30	64	94
1883	21	55	76
1884-1885	26	56	82
1891	7	7	14
1892-1893		6	6
1894	4	8	12
1895		14	14
1896	20	53	73
1897	30	47	77
1898	28	29	57
1900	30	40	70
1907	10	18	28
1908	42	54	96
1909	44	60	104
1910	31	30	61
1911	20	7	27
1912	23	34	57
1913	33	68	101

Comment 1913 INC.JEWEL

FRIENDSHIP AND PROSPER   ST.HILARY, CORNWALL   0163

Production: Copper	Ore(tons)	Metal(tons)	Value(£)
1852	124.00	5.20	384.00

Comment 1852 (C)

 FRIENDSHIP,EAST   MARYTAVY   SX 519794 0164

Production: Copper	Ore(tons)	Metal(tons)	Value(£)
1846	1135.00	139.00	8994.90
1847	2790.00	388.10	22756.50
1848	2787.00	346.60	20666.00
1852	2048.00	198.70	17263.20
1854	1396.00	127.00	13303.00

Comment 1846-1848 (C); 1853-1854 (C) FRIENDSHIP EAST

 FRIENDSHIP,NORTH   MARYTAVY   SX 512823 0165

Production: Lead & Silver	Ore(tons)	Lead(tons)	Silver(ozs)	Value(£)
1854	51.00	32.30		
1855	96.50	70.00	826.00	
1856	95.00	53.00	645.00	
1857	77.00	43.00	157.00	

Lead & Silver	Ore(tons)	Lead(tons)	Silver(ozs)	Value(£)
1858	37.80	28.50	285.00	
1859	17.00	13.00	143.00	
1860	No detailed return			
1861	7.10	4.20		

Copper No detailed return
Tin No detailed return

Ownership: Comment 1863-1865 SUSPENDED
Management: Chief Agent 1859-1862 Z.WILLIAMS & F.KENT
Secretary 1859-1865 JOS.MATTHEWS (P)

FRIENDSHIP,WEST   BRENTOR   SX 485796 0166

Production: Copper	Ore(tons)	Metal(tons)	Value(£)
1856	177.00	9.30	842.90

Comment 1856 (C)
Ownership: Comment 1862-1865 SUSPENDED
Management: Chief Agent 1861 J.H.HITCHENS
Secretary 1861-1865 H.DENDY (P)

FULLABROOK   BRAUNTON   SS 515398 0167

Production: Manganese	Ore(tons)	Metal(tons)	Value(£)
1884	100.00		200.00
1885	No detailed return		

Ownership: 1877 JOS.POPE; 1878-1881 H.J.MCCULLOCH & CO.; 1882-1884
JOS.POPE
Comment 1877-1881 SEE ALSO FULLABROOK,SOMERSET; 1884 NOT
WORKED IN 1884
Management: Chief Agent 1877-1884 JOS.POPE
Secretary 1878 JOS.POPE

Employment:	Underground	Surface	Total
1878	6	3	9
1879	4	5	9
1880		1	1
1881	1	1	2
1882	6	5	11
1883	4	2	6

FURGAM HILL   0168

Production: Iron	Ore(tons)	Iron(%)	Value(£)
1866	636.40		

Comment 1866 BH.FOR VALUE SEE DREWS

FURSDON   OKEHAMPTON   SX 650930 0169

Production: Copper	Ore(tons)	Metal(tons)	Value(£)
1861	175.00	11.30	1036.20

Copper	Ore(tons)	Metal(tons)	Value(£)
1862	359.00	24.70	2043.80
1863	311.00	15.70	1192.60
1864	344.00	16.20	1352.30
1865	444.00	19.90	1532.10
1866	193.00	14.40	997.90
1867	209.00	15.60	1140.90
1868	47.00	2.70	191.20
1869	135.00	6.50	385.60
1870	100.00	6.50	407.50
1872	789.00	41.80	3164.50
1873	1203.00	69.70	4404.90
1874	134.00	5.90	316.30
1875	94.00	7.70	580.50
1877	No detailed return		

Comment 1861-1870 (C); 1872-1875 (S); 1877 SEE EMILY

Ownership: Comment 1872-1875 FURSDON GREAT CONSOLS; 1876 NOW EMILY;
1877-1881 SEE EMILY

Management: Manager 1872 JOHN EDWARDS; 1873 M.ERN.JOBLING; 1874
IS.JACOBS; 1875 J.CROCKER; 1876 M.ERN.JOBLING
Chief Agent 1860 JOHN CORNISH; 1861-1867 J.COLLINS; 1868-1870
J.G.MARTIN; 1872-1874 JOHN CROCKER
Secretary 1860-1863 JAS.HAMPTON (P); 1864-1867 JOHN HITCHINS;
1869-1870 JOS.MATTHEWS; 1872 M.ERN.JOBLING; 1873 WM.BATTYE;
1874-1875 M.E.JOBLING&W.BATTYE; 1876 WM.BATTYE

✳ FURZE HILL   HORRABRIDGE   SX 516692 0170 ✳

Production: Copper No detailed return

Tin	Black(tons)	Stuff(tons)	Tin(tons)	Value(£)
1862	4.20			275.00
1863	2.50			168.70
1864	28.00			1717.50
1865	19.60			1087.00
1866	21.20			1053.90
1867	17.10			868.80
1868	4.50			212.30
1869	1.60			96.60
1870	2.10			128.70
1871	0.80			47.50
1872	7.80			610.60
1873	19.10			1435.30
1874	53.80			3031.60
1875	47.80			2550.20
1876	7.70			339.00
1877	2.10			81.60

Comment 1862 FURZE HILL WOOD-PART YEAR; 1863-1866 FURZE HILL
WOOD; 1867-1871 FURZE HILL WOOD CONSOLS; 1872-1873 FURZE HILL
WOOD

Arsenic	Ore(tons)	Metal(tons)	Value(£)
1875	1.80		2.50

Ownership: 1860 JAS.HAMPTON (P); 1870 THOS.HORSWILL

Comment 1860-1866 FURZE HILL WOOD CONSOLS; 1868 FURZE HILL
WOOD; 1870-1871 FURZE HILL WOOD; 1877-1879 SEE FURZE HILL,
SOMERSET
Management: Manager 1861-1863 THOS.GREGORY; 1864-1866 WM.DOIDGE;
1873-1875 WM.DOIDGE; 1880 WM.DOIDGE
Chief Agent 1860 C.THOMAS; 1861-1863 F.POMEROY; 1870
WM.DOIDGE; 1871-1872 WM.DOIDGE & ED.BETTELEY
Secretary 1860-1861 W.POPE JNR. (P); 1862-1863 W.BETTELEY;
1864-1866 THOS.HORSWILL; 1870 ED.BETTELEY; 1871-1875
THOS.HORSWILL (S); 1880 WM.DOIDGE

FURZE HILL,WEST   HORRABRIDGE   0171

Production: Tin No detailed return
Management: Manager 1872 WM.DOIDGE
Chief Agent 1873 ED.BETTELEY

FURZE PARK   LEWTRENCHARD   0172

Production: Copper	Ore(tons)	Metal(tons)	Value(£)
1862	5.00	0.60	52.00
1863	5.00	0.70	54.20

Comment 1862-1863 (C)
Manganese No detailed return
Ownership: Comment 1860-1867 SEE LEW WOOD

FURZEHAM   BRIXHAM   0173

Production: Iron	Ore(tons)	Iron(%)	Value(£)
1874	1300.00		965.00

Comment 1874 HE.TWO RETURNS AGGREGATED
Ownership: 1873-1875 WM.BROWNE
Comment 1873 FURSEHAM
Management: Manager 1873-1875 PHAR.GROSE
Chief Agent 1874-1875 J.H.PEARSON

GAWTON   TAVISTOCK   SX 452689 0174

Production: Copper	Ore(tons)	Metal(tons)	Value(£)
1857	349.00	14.80	1361.90
1858	415.00	13.80	1019.80
1859	318.00	11.50	933.40
1860	233.00	8.20	638.60
1861	199.00	8.50	675.50
1862	213.00	13.10	964.30
1863	94.00	3.20	213.80
1866	745.00	39.50	2429.20
1867	1224.00	59.30	4011.70
1868	1062.00	49.20	3241.20

Copper	Ore(tons)	Metal(tons)	Value(£)
1869	1000.00	54.60	3363.60
1870	1274.00	75.30	4393.00
1871	1376.00	76.00	4787.20
1872	1846.00	80.40	5900.20
1873	1061.00	52.80	3169.90
1874	533.00	24.20	1391.20
1875	720.00	34.50	2559.80
1876	1061.00	42.90	2639.60
1877	1126.00	44.10	2296.80
1878	789.60	33.60	1458.10
1879	547.10	19.50	781.20
1880	273.20	11.00	541.90
1881	242.70	11.10	629.40
1882	1143.60	51.40	2287.00
1883	814.70	8.50	520.00
1884	541.00		226.00
1885	224.00		78.00
1888	166.00		260.00
1889	112.00		42.00
1890	331.00		414.00
1891	113.00		179.00
1892	16.00		33.00
1894	36.00		21.00
1896	58.00		14.00
1899	153.00		68.00
1900	1.00		33.00
1901	6.00		40.00
1902	13.00		43.00

Comment 1857–1860 (C) GAWTON COPPER MINES; 1861–1863 (C);
1866–1873 (C); 1874 (C) GAWTON COPPER MINES; 1875–1876 (C)

Tin	Black(tons)	Stuff(tons)	Tin(tons)	Value(£)
1853	22.00			1705.10

Comment 1853 GAWTON UNITED

Arsenic	Ore(tons)	Metal(tons)	Value(£)
1867	56.30		38.00
1882	796.00		3184.00
1883	849.00		5250.00
1884	845.80		5286.00
1885	907.30		5885.00
1886	807.70		4789.00
1887	825.00		5377.00
1888	928.00		6555.00
1889	681.00		5013.00
1890	554.00		4430.00
1891	700.00		7326.00
1892	371.00		3511.00
1893	259.00		2851.00
1894	473.00		5228.00
1895	1103.00		13428.00
1896	615.00		8308.00
1897	1059.00		20533.00
1898	1041.00		14538.00

63

Arsenic	Ore(tons)	Metal(tons)	Value(£)
1899	1139.00		18932.00
1900	1304.00		23608.00
1901	950.00		13197.00
1902	223.00		2690.00

Comment 1867 CRUDE ARSENIC; 1884-1885 SOOT; 1886 CRUDE

Arsenic Pyrite	Ore(tons)	Value(£)
1874	377.50	391.90
1876	298.00	283.50
1877	525.50	2133.00
1878	234.00	163.10
1879	1481.70	1199.50
1880	334.00	391.90
1889	150.00	75.00
1891	127.00	32.00

Comment 1876 ARSENICAL MUNDIC

Ownership: 1877-1884 GAWTON COPPER MINING CO.; 1885-1886 GAWTON MINING CO.; 1887-1895 GAWTON MINING CO.LTD.; 1896-1903 DEVON GAWTON MINING CO.LTD.

Comment 1860-1862 GAWTON UNITED; 1863-1870 GAWTON COPPER; 1881 NOT WORKED; 1902 IN LIQUIDATION; 1903 SUSPENDED

Management: Manager 1870-1881 GEO.ROWE
Chief Agent 1859-1869 GEO.ROWE; 1870-1879 G.ROWE JNR.; 1881 GEO.ROWE JNR.; 1882-1903 GEO.ROWE
Secretary 1859-1864 WM.WATSON (P); 1865-1866 W.E.CUMMINS; 1867 WM.WATSON; 1868-1871 MOSES BAWDEN; 1872-1876 JAS.HICKEY; 1877 J.HICKEY & M.BAWDEN(P); 1878 MOSES BAWDEN (P); 1879-1881 S.HICKEY (P); 1887-1902 MOSES BAWDEN

Employment:	Underground	Surface	Total
1878	24	34	58
1879	33	27	60
1880	26	58	84
1881	18	68	86
1882	40	58	98
1883	76	49	125
1884	42	48	90
1885	33	41	74
1886	36	46	82
1887	36	44	80
1888	32	50	82
1889	41	41	82
1890	39	53	92
1891	33	62	95
1892	4	26	30
1893	33	67	100
1894	44	80	124
1895	74	118	192
1896	84	119	203
1897	96	172	268
1898	94	134	228
1900	85	117	202
1901	57	94	151
1902	10	36	46

GEM

WHITCHURCH   SX 496706 0175 ✱

Production: Tin	Black(tons)	Stuff(tons)	Tin(tons)	Value(£)
1871	11.20			845.40
1872	11.50			1013.80
1873	6.70			536.50
1874	1.60			87.80

Ownership: Comment 1871 GEW
Management: Chief Agent 1871-1873 RICH.UNSWORTH; 1874 JOHN GOLDSWORTHY
Secretary 1871 W.CRIPER; 1872-1873 JOHN GOLDSWORTHY

GEORGE,EAST

SAMPFORD SPINEY   SX 529703 0176 ✱

Production: Copper	Ore(tons)	Metal(tons)	Value(£)
1853	165.00	13.90	1356.20
1854	163.00	10.40	994.30
1855	115.00	6.80	655.00

Comment 1853-1855 (C)

GIRT DOWN

COMBE MARTIN   SS 603485 0177

Production: Iron	Ore(tons)	Iron(%)	Value(£)
1873	100.00		75.00
1874	300.00		180.00

Comment 1873-1874 BH.
Ownership: 1873-1876 J.D.JORDAN
Comment 1875-1876 GIRT & HOLSTON DOWN
Management: Chief Agent 1874 WM.PARKIN; 1875-1876 H.A.HOLDEN

GOBBETT

HEXWORTHY   SX 647728 0178 ✱

Production: Tin	Black(tons)	Stuff(tons)	Tin(tons)	Value(£)
1873	0.90			70.00
1874	1.50			85.00

Comment 1873 VALUE EST.
Ownership: 1881-1884 JAS.BROWNING & OTHERS
Comment 1883 NOT WORKED IN 1883
Management: Manager 1873-1875 JAS.BROWNING
Chief Agent 1881-1884 JAS.BROWNING

Employment:	Underground	Surface	Total
1881	5		5
1884	4		4

GOLDEN DAGGER

MANATON   SX 680803 0179

Production: Tin	Black(tons)	Stuff(tons)	Tin(tons)	Value(£)
1882	0.50		0.30	26.00
1883	1.40			85.00
1884	1.00			44.00
1886	9.10			562.00
1887	6.60			434.00

Tin	Black(tons)	Stuff(tons)	Tin(tons)	Value(£)
1888	6.20			458.00
1889	15.50			922.00
1890	14.10			822.00
1892	25.60			1530.00
1893	14.50			722.00
1894	6.20			273.00
1895	17.00			672.00
1896	1.50			53.00
1897	0.80			29.00
1898	1.50		1.00	69.00
1899	3.00		2.00	210.00
1900	7.30			581.00
1901	8.00			566.00
1902	7.00			493.00
1903	5.10			389.00
1904	2.00			162.00
1905	1.00			88.00
1906	2.20			295.00
1907	11.30			1180.00
1908	6.00			489.00
1909	3.30			281.00
1910	10.00			915.00
1911	11.30			1461.00
1912	13.50			1944.00
1913	9.00			990.00

Ownership: 1880-1890 MOSES BAWDEN; 1891 GOLDEN DAGGER TIN MINE
SYNDICATE; 1903-1904 BAWDEN & CO.; 1905-1908 DARTMOOR
MINERALS LTD.; 1909-1913 GOLDEN DAGGER MINE LTD.
Comment 1885 NOT WORKED IN 1885; 1908 IN LIQUIDATION; 1913
TECHNICAL ADVISER = C.G.MOOR
Management: Manager 1909-1912 THOS.SETTLE
Chief Agent 1866 M.DUNN; 1880-1881 GEO.G.ROWE JNR.; 1891-1904
MOSES BAWDEN
Secretary 1880-1902 MOSES BAWDEN; 1910-1911 H.MACHONOCHIE

Employment:

	Underground	Surface	Total
1880		6	6
1881-1882	6	2	8
1883	4	2	6
1884	4		4
1886	6	8	14
1887	10	5	15
1888	10	4	14
1889	10	6	16
1890	8	4	12
1891	12	16	28
1892	23	18	41
1893	14	18	32
1894	10	10	20
1895	9	13	22
1896	6	2	8
1897	6	4	10
1898	2	2	4

GOLDEN DAGGER   MANATON   Continued

	Underground	Surface	Total
1900-1901	8	2	10
1902	6	2	8
1903	7	2	9
1904	4	2	6
1905	6	5	11
1906	66	51	117
1907-1908	4	2	6
1909	5	2	7
1910	10	8	18
1911	14	6	20
1912	20	8	28
1913	12	5	17

GOODRINGTON   PAIGNTON   0180

Production: Iron No detailed return
Ownership: 1873-1874 WM.BROWNE; 1875-1876 WM.BROWNE & SONS
Management: Manager 1873-1876 PHAR.GROSE

GOOSEFORD,WEST   THROWLEIGH   SX 672925 0181

Production: Tin No detailed return
Ownership: 1907-1911 DEFRIES & SONS LTD.
     Comment 1909 SUSPENDED; 1910 NO MINERAL RETURNED IN 1910;
     1911 ABANDONED
Employment:

	Underground	Surface	Total
1908	13	10	23
1910		2	2

GREAT ROCK   HENNOCK   SX 827815 0182

Production: Iron

	Ore(tons)	Iron(%)	Value(£)
1902	87.00		
1903	100.00		
1904	100.00		
1905	100.00		
1906	142.00		
1907	120.00		
1908	122.00		
1909	162.00		
1910	140.00		
1911	205.00		
1912	266.00		
1913	350.00		

     Comment 1902-1913 MICACEOUS HAEMATITE,RETURNED AS UMBER
Ownership: 1896-1899 OTTO SCHMIDT & CO.; 1900-1901 G GARTZKE & CO.;
     1902-1913 FERRUBRON MANUFACTURING CO.
Management: Chief Agent 1896-1913 W.H.HOSKING
     Secretary 1896-1913 W.H.HOSKING

GREAT ROCK   HENNOCK   Continued

Employment: Underground   Surface   Total
                1896   4   4
                1901   2   2
                1902   4   3   7
                1903   4   4   8
                1904   6   3   9
                1905   4   3   7
                1906   4   2   6
                1907   4   4   8
                1908-1909   4   2   6
                1910   5   3   8
                1911   4   5   9
                1912   6   8   14
                1913   6   11   17

GREAT WEEK CONSOLS   GREAT WEEKE   SX 713875 0183

Production: Tin   Black(tons) Stuff(tons)   Tin(tons)   Value(£)
                1887   3.50   295.00
                1888   22.20   1421.00
                1889   19.20   1087.00
                1890   8.90   476.00
                1891   1.20   67.00
Ownership: 1886-1890 GREAT WEEK CONSOLS ADVENTURERS; 1891-1895 GREAT
            WEEK MINE CO.
            Comment 1886 GREAT WEEK
Management: Chief Agent 1891-1894 SML.LEACH
            Secretary 1886 CHAS.H.MAUNDER; 1887-1890 SML.LEACH; 1891-1894
            GEO.LEACH (P)
Employment: Underground   Surface   Total
                1886   6   6
                1887   14   24   38
                1888   17   18   35
                1889   10   10   20
                1890   4   3   7
                1891   1   1

GUNNISLAKE   GUNNISLAKE, CORNWALL   SX 421720 0184

Production: Copper   Ore(tons) Metal(tons)   Value(£)
                1859   337.00   26.80   2546.40

GUNNISLAKE,EAST   GUNNISLAKE, CORNWALL   SX 423718 0185

Production: Copper   Ore(tons) Metal(tons)   Value(£)
            1855-1858 No detailed return
                1859   135.00   6.00   587.10
                1865   No detailed return
                1868   No detailed return
                1870   No detailed return

68

GUNNISLAKE,EAST   GUNNISLAKE, CORNWALL   Continued

                  Copper   Ore(tons) Metal(tons)   Value(£)
                  1873   No detailed return
                  Comment 1855-1856 SEE SOUTH BEDFORD; 1858 SEE SOUTH BEDFORD;
                  1859 (C); 1865 SEE EAST GUNNISLAKE, CORNWALL; 1868 SEE EAST
                  GUNNISLAKE, CORNWALL; 1870 SEE EAST GUNNISLAKE, CORNWALL;
                  1873 SEE EAST GUNNISLAKE, CORNWALL
                  Tin   Black(tons) Stuff(tons)   Tin(tons)   Value(£)
                  1860   1.10   70.50
                  1862   1.00   48.50
                  Comment 1860 INC.SOUTH BEDFORD; 1862 INC.SOUTH BEDFORD
Ownership: Comment 1859-1875 SEE SOUTH BEDFORD

GUNNISLAKE,OLD   GUNNISLAKE, CORNWALL   SX 430719 0186

Production: Tin   Black(tons) Stuff(tons)   Tin(tons)   Value(£)
            1866   1.00   31.60

GYMTON   PAIGNTON   0187

Production: Iron No detailed return
Ownership: 1864 JNO.SMITH; 1865-1868 BEN.SMITH; 1869-1872 JOHN BROGDEN &
            SON
Management: Chief Agent 1864 WM.GROSE; 1865-1868 JNO.BROKENSHIRE;
            1869-1872 JNO.SMITH

HARBOUR FORD   IVYBRIDGE   0188

Production: Iron No detailed return
Ownership: 1874 T.M.MATTHEWS
Management: Chief Agent 1874 T.M.MATTHEWS

HARRIS   LIFTON   SX 427813 0189

Production: Lead & Silver No detailed return
Ownership: Comment 1862-1865 SUSPENDED
Management: Chief Agent 1860 W.E.CUMMINS; 1861 JOHN PRYOR
            Secretary 1860 W.THOMPSON (P); 1861-1865 W.E.CUMMINS (P)

HATHERBY   ILSINGTON   0190

Production: Iron   Ore(tons)   Iron(%)   Value(£)
            1866   50.00   16.20
            1867   500.00   200.00
            Comment 1866-1867 MO.HATHERLEYS
Ownership: 1866-1870 WM.BROWNE
            Comment 1866-1869 MAGNETIC; 1870 MAGNETIC SUSPENDED
Management: Chief Agent 1866-1869 WM.GROSE

Production: Iron	Ore(tons)	Iron(%)	Value(£)
1892	36.00		144.00
1893	60.00		240.00
1894	230.00		1050.00
1895	230.00	49.00	1150.00
1896	273.00	49.00	1365.00
1897	194.00		1164.00
1898	60.00		
1899	40.00		
1900	40.00		
1901	40.00		
1902	10.00		

Comment 1892-1893 BH.HAWKMOOR SHINING ORE (MH); 1894-1895
BH.INC.SHAPTOR (MH); 1896 BH.INC.SHAPTOR & PLUMLEY (MH); 1897
BH.DITTO SHUTTAMOOR (MH); 1898-1902 MH.

Ownership: 1892-1899 OTTO SCHMIDT & CO.; 1900-1901 G.GARTZKE & CO.;
1902-1903 FERRUBRON MANUFACTURING CO.

Management: Chief Agent 1892-1902 W.H.HOSKING
Secretary 1892-1903 W.H.HOSKING

Employment:	Underground	Surface	Total
1892-1893	4	2	6
1894-1895	4	1	5
1896		1	1
1897-1898	2	1	3
1900-1901	2	1	3

Production: Manganese	Ore(tons)	Metal(tons)	Value(£)
1874	10.00		40.00

Production: Iron	Ore(tons)	Iron(%)	Value(£)
1874	20.00		25.00

Comment 1874 RH.

Production: Iron	Ore(tons)	Iron(%)	Value(£)
1858	3000.00		1420.00
1859	1293.50		612.00
1860	1356.00		542.40
1861	68.00		27.20
1865	2176.00		730.60
1866	60.00		19.50
1868	1127.80		338.30
1869	505.00		151.50
1870	No detailed return		
1871	200.00		150.00

Iron	Ore(tons)	Iron(%)	Value(£)
1872	3000.00		1800.00
1873	600.00		450.00
1874	1669.00		1500.00
1875	530.30		159.10
1876	1781.40		890.90
1877	2611.40		1305.70
1878	724.00		362.00
1879	150.00		75.00
1880	3395.00		2121.90
1881	3300.00		2887.50
1882	3840.00	57.00	3360.00
1883	No detailed return		
1908	1400.00	57.50	500.00
1910	2000.00	67.00	700.00

Comment 1858-1861 BH.INC.ILSINGTON; 1865 MO.HAYTOR VALE
INC.SMALLACOMBE; 1866 MO.HAYTOR VALE; 1868 MO.HAYTOR VALE;
1869-1871 MO.; 1872 MO.HAYTOR VALE; 1873 MO.; 1874 MO.BUT SEE
HAYTOR CORNWALL; 1875 MO.HAYTOR VALE; 1876-1883 MO.; 1908
MO.ILSINGTON(HAYTOR); 1910 MO.

Ownership: 1864-1868 WM.BROWNE; 1872-1876 WM.BROWNE; 1877 WM.BROWNE &
SONS; 1878 HAYTOR MAGNETIC IRON CO.LTD.; 1879-1881 HAYTOR
MAGNETIC IRON CO.; 1882-1883 HAYTOR MAGNETIC IRON ORE
CO.LTD.
Comment 1864-1868 HAYTOR VALE; 1872-1878 HAYTOR VALE;
1907-1913 SEE ILSINGTON

Management: Chief Agent 1864-1868 WM.GROSE; 1872-1877 WM.GROSE; 1878
F.WARWICK; 1879-1883 WM.GROSE
Secretary 1879-1880 F.WARWICK (S)

Employment:
	Underground	Surface	Total
1878	4	5	9
1880	64	28	92
1881	30	52	82
1882	28	45	73
1907	6	2	8
1908	10	15	25
1910	10	6	16

HAYTOR CONSOLS   ILSINGTON   SX 745761 0195

Production: Tin	Black(tons)	Stuff(tons)	Tin(tons)	Value(£)
1853	7.30			504.10
1854	6.20			338.50
1855	2.30			123.00

Comment 1855 HAYTON CONSOLS
Ownership: Comment 1862 HAYTOR TIN; 1863-1865 HAYTOR TIN SUSPENDED

HAZEL   ASHBURTON   SX 728710 0196

Production: Copper No detailed return
Tin No detailed return

HAZEL   ASHBURTON   Continued

Ownership: Comment 1862-1864 SUSPENDED

HAZEL MINE   ASHBURTON   SX 728710 0197

Production: Tin No detailed return
Ownership: Comment 1863-1865 SUSPENDED

HAZEL,EAST   ASHBURTON   0198

Production: Copper No detailed return
            Tin No detailed return
Ownership: Comment 1860-1865 SUSPENDED
Management: Secretary 1860-1865 F.P.JELLARD (P)

✳ HEALE   LIFTON   0199✳

Production: Manganese No detailed return
Management: Manager 1860-1867 JOHN SIMS
            Chief Agent 1860-1867 N.TRUSCOTT
            Secretary 1860-1867 JOHN SIMS (P); 1868-1872 C.JOHN SIMS &
            F.SIMS

HEMERDON CONSOLS   PLYMPTON   SX 572588 0200

Production: Tin   Black(tons) Stuff(tons) Tin(tons)   Value(£)
            1855   15.20   820.00
            1856   7.10   467.30
Ownership: Comment 1874-1875 HAMERDON CONSOLS
Management: Manager 1871-1872 HY.MINERS; 1874-1875 HY.MINERS
            Chief Agent 1873 HY.MINERS
            Secretary 1871 JOHN ARNOLD; 1872-1875 W.H.B.KEMPE

HENNOCK   HENNOCK   SX 836814 0201

Production: Lead & Silver Ore(tons) Lead(tons) Silver(ozs) Value(£)
            1853   29.00   21.00   36.00
            Iron   Ore(tons)   Iron(%)   Value(£)
            1872   181.00   60.80
            Comment 1872 MH.
Ownership: 1870-1873 VAN IRON ORE CO.
            Comment 1863-1865 OLD HENNOCK SUSPENDED
Management: Chief Agent 1870-1873 W.H.HOSKING

✳ HENRY   LIFTON   0202✳

Production: Manganese No detailed return
Management: Chief Agent 1860 JOHN SIMS; 1861-1866 C.JOHN SIMS

Secretary 1860-1866 JOHN SIMS

✳ HEXWORTHY   HEXWORTHY   SX 655710 0203 ✳

Production: Tin	Black(tons)	Stuff(tons)	Tin(tons)	Value(£)
1891	18.30			1110.00
1892	52.00			3150.00
1893	30.50			1709.00
1894	24.00			1100.00
1895	8.40			3.10
1896	2.50			105.00
1908	47.50			4196.00
1909	6.80			572.00
1910	6.70			659.00
1911	0.60			79.00
1912	0.40			54.00

Ownership: 1889-1896 HEXWORTHY TIN MINING CO.LTD.; 1897 E.H.BAYLDON;
1905-1909 DARTMOOR MINERALS LTD.; 1910 GOLDEN DAGGER MINE
CO.; 1911-1913 D.B.SYNDICATE PER H.MACONOCHIE
Comment 1897 ABANDONED 1897; 1908-1913 IN LIQUIDATION
Management: Chief Agent 1889-1896 JOHN WEBB
Secretary 1889-1890 ED.MOGRIDGE; 1891-1894 JOHN GARLAND (S)

Employment:	Underground	Surface	Total
1889	10	6	16
1890	22	14	36
1891	30	29	59
1892	37	21	58
1893	33	20	53
1894	6	2	8
1895	2		2
1896	12	5	17
1905		6	6
1906		15	15
1907	25	19	44
1908	26	19	45
1909	13	9	22
1910	8	5	13
1911	4	2	6
1912	2	1	3
1913		3	3

✳ HOGSTOR   MILTON ABBOT   SX 431812 0204 ✳

Production: Manganese	Ore(tons)	Metal(tons)	Value(£)
1858-1860 No detailed return			
1867-1868 No detailed return			
1870-1888 No detailed return			
1890-1895 No detailed return			
1902-1907 No detailed return			

Comment 1858-1860 HOGSTON SEE CHILLATON; 1867 HOGSTON SEE
CHILLATON; 1868 SEE CHILLATON; 1870-1880 SEE CHILLATON; 1881

HOGSTON SEE CHILLATON; 1882-1888 SEE CHILLATON; 1890-1895 SEE
CHILLATON; 1902-1907 SEE CHILLATON
Ownership: Comment 1872-1878 SEE CHILLATON; 1880-1887 SEE CHILLATON;
1890 SEE CHILLATON; 1901-1909 SEE CHILLATON
Management: Chief Agent 1867 C.JOHN SIMS; 1868-1871 C.JOHN SIMS & F.SIMS
Secretary 1867 JOHN SIMS; 1868-1871 C.JOHN SIMS & F.SIMS

Employment: Underground   Surface   Total
            1878
            1880-1886
            1890
            1901-1909
            Comment 1878 SEE CHILLATON; 1880-1886 SEE CHILLATON; 1890 SEE
            CHILLATON; 1901-1909 SEE CHILLATON

HOLNE CHASE   ASHBURTON   SX 723715 0205

Production:	Tin	Black(tons)	Stuff(tons)	Tin(tons)	Value(£)
	1875	4.80			253.80

Comment 1875 HOLME CHASE
Ownership: 1877-1878 G.A.MALCOLM
Management: Chief Agent 1874-1875 E.F.BEAN; 1876-1878 HY.TREGANOWAN
Secretary 1874-1875 G.A.MALCOLM & E.F.BEAN; 1876-1877
G.A.MALCOLM

Employment:		Underground	Surface	Total
	1878	5	1	6

HOLNE MOOR   ASHBURTON   SX 675698 0206

Production:	Tin	Black(tons)	Stuff(tons)	Tin(tons)	Value(£)
	1854	0.50			22.60
	1855	0.60			38.10

HOLSTON DOWN   COMBE MARTIN   0207

Production: Iron No detailed return
Ownership: 1873-1874 J.D.JORDAN
            Comment 1875-1876 SEE GIRT DOWN

✳ HOOE,NORTH   BERE ALSTON   SX 427661 0208 ✳

Production: Lead No detailed return
            Tin No detailed return
Ownership: 1905-1906 DEVON MINING SYNDICATE
            Comment 1905 NORTH HOVE; 1906 SUSPENDED
Management: Chief Agent 1905-1906 DUD.J.C.BUSH

Employment:		Underground	Surface	Total
	1905		8	8

HOOK HILL   0209

Production: Iron   Ore(tons)   Iron(%)   Value(£)
            1870   896.00   448.00
            Comment 1870 BH.

HUCKWORTHY BRIDGE   TAVISTOCK   SX 533707 0210

Production: Copper No detailed return
Ownership: Comment 1862-1865 SUSPENDED
Management: Manager 1860-1861 WM.CLEMO
            Chief Agent 1860-1861 HY.RODDA
            Secretary 1860-1865 W.E.CUMMINS (P)

HUNTINGDON   ASHBURTON   SX 666673 0211

Production: Tin No detailed return
Ownership: Comment 1863-1867 SEE DEVON CONSOLS
Management: Chief Agent 1862 MART.DOWN

ILSINGTON   ILSINGTON   SX 773771 0212

Production: Iron   Ore(tons)   Iron(%)   Value(£)
            1858-1861 No detailed return
            1872   2000.00   1500.00
            1908   No detailed return
            Comment 1858-1861 MO.SEE HAYTOR; 1872 MO.; 1908 MO.SEE
            HAYTOR
Ownership: 1907-1913 ILSINGTON MINING CO.LTD.
            Comment 1907-1908 OR HAYTOR; 1909 OR HAYTOR SUSPENDED; 1910
            OR HAYTOR; 1911-1913 OR HAYTOR SUSPENDED DEC.1910

IVY TOR   SOUTH TAWTON   SX 628936 0213

Production: Copper No detailed return
Management: Chief Agent 1860-1867 J.P.DAW
            Secretary 1860-1867 A.WHIPPAM (P)

IVYBRIDGE   IVYBRIDGE   SX 647551 0214

Production: Lead & Silver   Ore(tons) Lead(tons) Silver(ozs) Value(£)
            1855   149.50   96.00   2688.00
            1856   134.90   75.00
            1857   No detailed return
            Zinc   Ore(tons) Metal(tons) Value(£)
            1855   No detailed return
            Comment 1855 SEE GREAT WHEAL BADDERN (CORNWALL)

                                    75

Production: Copper No detailed return

Tin	Black(tons) Stuff(tons)	Tin(tons)	Value(£)
1913	No detailed return		

Comment 1913 SEE FRIENDSHIP

Arsenic	Ore(tons)	Metal(tons)	Value(£)
1913	28.70		359.00

Comment 1913 INC FRIENDSHIP

Ownership: 1913 WHEAL JEWELL & MARY TAVY MINES LTD.
Comment 1862-1865 SUSPENDED; 1913 REOPENED APRIL 1912

Management: Manager 1859-1861 Z.WILLIAMS; 1913 MURRAY
Chief Agent 1859 F.KENT
Secretary 1859-1865 JOS.MATTHEWS (P); 1913 BROWNING &
FLEMING

Employment:	Underground	Surface	Total
1913			

Comment 1913 SEE FRIENDSHIP

JULIAN   PLYMPTON   SX 551597 0216

Production: Tin No detailed return
Ownership: Comment 1862-1865 SUSPENDED
Management: Chief Agent 1860-1861 WM.EDWARDS
Secretary 1860-1865 H.WILLS (P)

KELLY   LUSTLEIGH   SX 795818 0217

Production: Iron	Ore(tons)	Iron(%)	Value(£)
1879	20.00		10.00
1880	22.00		66.00
1881	25.00		75.00
1882	30.00	50.00	90.00
1883	20.00		60.00
1884	20.00		40.00
1885	20.00		40.00
1886	22.00		66.00
1887	30.00		
1888	25.00		6.00
1889	30.00		3.00
1890	30.00		90.00
1891	30.00		90.00
1901	20.00		
1902	80.00		
1903	50.00		
1904	122.00		
1905	180.00		
1906	160.00		
1907	202.00		
1908	70.00		
1909	197.00		
1910	185.00		
1911	88.00		

Iron	Ore(tons)	Iron(%)	Value(£)
1912	165.00		
1913	170.00		

Comment 1879–1891 BH. (MH); 1901 BH. (MH); 1902–1913
MICACEOUS HAEMATITE,RETURNED AS UMBER

Ownership: 1877 KELLY IRON CO.; 1879 W.H.HOSKING; 1880–1881 KELLEY IRON
MINES CO.; 1882–1892 W.H.HOSKING; 1900–1913 SCOTTISH SILVOID
CO.LTD.
Comment 1879 KOLLEY; 1880–1881 KELLEY; 1892 SUSPENDED
THROUGHOUT 1892

Management: Chief Agent 1877 W.H.HOSKING; 1879–1892 W.H.HOSKING;
1900–1913 A.W.GOVAN

Employment:

	Underground	Surface	Total
1879–1880	1	1	2
1881	2	1	3
1882	1	1	2
1883	2		2
1884	2	1	3
1885	2		2
1886	1	1	2
1887	1		1
1888–1889	1	1	2
1890	2		2
1891	1	1	2
1901	8	5	13
1902	6	2	8
1903	2		2
1904	6	4	10
1905	6	3	9
1906	4	3	7
1907–1908	4	4	8
1909	6	5	11
1910	4	3	7
1911	5	2	7
1912	4	4	8
1913	4	5	9

KINGS OVEN & WATERHILL   NORTH BOVEY   SX 674813 0218

Production: Tin No detailed return
Management: Manager 1869–1872 WM.SKEWIS
Secretary 1869–1872 D.COHEN

KIT   SHEEPSTOR   SX 563675 0219

Production: Tin No detailed return
Ownership: 1901–1904 KIT TIN MINES LTD.
Comment 1903 SUSPENDED
Management: Chief Agent 1901–1904 ALF.THOMAS
Employment:

	Underground	Surface	Total
1901	8	7	15

	Underground	Surface	Total
1902	9		9
1903	8	7	15
1904	10		10

✷ KITTY   POSTBRIDGE   0220✷

Ownership: 1887 ED.MOGRIDGE
Management: Chief Agent 1887 JOHN WEBB

LADOCK   LADOCK, CORNWALL   SW 915525 0221

Production: Iron No detailed return
Ownership: 1871 WELSH IRON WORKS
Management: Chief Agent 1871 W.H.HOSKING

✷ LAMERHOOE   LAMERTON   SX 395738 0222✷

Production: Lead & Silver	Ore(tons)	Lead(tons)	Silver(ozs)	Value(£)
1854	15.00	11.20	135.00	

Comment 1854 LAMERHOSE

LANGFORD   NEWTON ST.CYRES   SX 901978 0223

Production: Manganese No detailed return
Ownership: 1889-1891 LANGFORD MANGANESE CO.LTD.
           Comment 1890 IN LIQUIDATION
Management: Chief Agent 1889 JOS.POPE; 1890 JOHN NEEP
           Secretary 1891 JOHN NEEP

Employment:	Underground	Surface	Total
1889	6	14	20
1890		11	11

✷ LANGSTONE   LAMERTON   SX 483826 0224 >

Production: Manganese	Ore(tons)	Metal(tons)	Value(£)
1874	50.00		250.00
1890	10.00		10.00

Ownership: 1879-1880 C.DE VALHERMY; 1881-1883 WEST OF ENGLAND MINING
           CO.LTD.; 1885-1887 J.BAILEY & OTHERS
           Comment 1872 LONGSTONE; 1874 SEE LANGSTONE, CORNWALL; 1880
           NOT WORKED; 1883 NOT WORKED IN 1883
Management: Manager 1875-1876 N.H.NICHOLLS
           Chief Agent 1872 THOS.GREGORY; 1879-1880 C.DE VALHERMY; 1881
           WM.DOIDGE
           Secretary 1872 JOHN LOMAS; 1885-1887 J.BAILEY

Employment:	Underground	Surface	Total
1879	8		8

LANGSTONE   LAMERTON   Continued

	Underground	Surface	Total
1881	18	10	28
1882	16	7	23
1885	13	2	15
1886	24	15	39

✳LEE WOOD   SYDENHAM DAMEREL   SX 438837 0225 ✳

Production: Manganese   Ore(tons) Metal(tons)   Value(£)
            1870-1871 No detailed return
            Comment 1870-1871 SEE SYDENHAM

✳ LEW TRENCHARD   LEW TRENCHARD   SX 457846 0226 ✳

Production: Manganese   Ore(tons) Metal(tons)   Value(£)
            1858-1860 No detailed return
            1867   No detailed return
            Comment 1858-1860 LOW TRENCHARD SEE CHILLATON; 1867 SEE
            CHILLATON
Management: Chief Agent 1875-1877 JOHN GOLDSWORTHY
            Secretary 1875-1877 J.S.JOHNSON

✳ LEW WOOD   LEW TRENCHARD   0227 ✳

Production: Manganese No detailed return
Ownership: Comment 1860-1861 LECO WOOD OR FURZE PARK; 1862-1867
            INC.FURZE PARK
Management: Manager 1860-1867 JOHN SIMS; 1868-1872 C.JOHN SIMS & F.SIMS
            Chief Agent 1860-1872 N.TRUSCOTT
            Secretary 1860-1867 JOHN SIMS; 1868-1872 C.JOHN SIMS &
            F.SIMS

✳LIFTON   LIFTON   0228 ✳

Production: Manganese   Ore(tons) Metal(tons)   Value(£)
            1858-1860 No detailed return
            1867   No detailed return
            Comment 1858-1859 LIFTON MINES SEE CHILLATON; 1860 SEE
            CHILLATON; 1867 SEE CHILLATON
Ownership: Comment 1873 STOPPED 1873
Management: Manager 1873-1875 WM.DOIDGE
            Chief Agent 1862-1871 C.JOHN SIMS; 1872 C.JOHN SIMS &
            I.JACKSON
            Secretary 1862-1867 JOHN SIMS; 1868-1872 C.JOHN SIMS &
            F.SIMS; 1873-1875 SIMS BROS.

✳ LUCKY   WALKHAMPTON   SX 583735 0229➔

Production: Tin No detailed return
Management: Chief Agent 1873-1877 JOHN GOLDSWORTHY
            Secretary 1873-1877 JAS.J.COWELL

✳ LYDFORD CONSOLS   LYDFORD   SX 517846 0230➔

Production: Lead & Silver   Ore(tons) Lead(tons) Silver(ozs)   Value(£)
            1848   4.00   2.00
            1849   No detailed return
            1879   6.80   5.50   50.00   71.00
            Tin No detailed return
Ownership: 1878-1881 SML.MAYNE
            Comment 1862-1865 SUSPENDED
Management: Manager 1860-1861 WM.SKEWIS; 1879-1881 SML.MAYNE
            Secretary 1860-1865 JOHN BAYLY & SON (P)
Employment: Underground   Surface   Total
            1879   3   2   5

MAEX,SOUTH   BRADDA,ISLE OF MAN   0231

Production: Lead   Ore(tons) Metal(tons)   Value(£)
            1850   25.00   17.00
            1851   No detailed return

MARCIA   TWITCHEN   SS 787301 0232

Production: Iron   Ore(tons)   Iron(%)   Value(£)
            1875   200.00   150.00
            1876   200.00   120.00
            Comment 1875-1876 BH.
Ownership: 1873-1874 THOS.J.SPENCE; 1875-1876 MARCIA HAEMATITE IRON
            MINING CO.LTD.
Management: Chief Agent 1873-1874 FRED.MITCHELL; 1875-1876 THOS.J.SPENCE

✳ MARIA   TAVISTOCK   SX 417738 0233➔

Production: Copper   Ore(tons) Metal(tons)   Value(£)
    -       1845   11288.00   1484.30   100971.80
            1846   15684.00   1578.40   95469.50
            1847   14175.00   1474.60   95873.10
            1857   310.00   84.70   9409.00
            1858   746.00   219.60   21710.00
            1859   1300.00   341.70   34800.00
            1860   1397.00   354.00   35274.10
            1861   816.00   177.30   16536.80
            Comment 1845-1847 (C); 1857-1861 (S)

MARIA,EAST   OKEHAMPTON   SX 413740 0234 ✳

Production: Copper No detailed return
Management: Chief Agent 1860-1868 C.WILLIAMS
            Secretary 1860-1868 R.SARJEANT (P)

✳ MARIA,WEST   LAMERTON   SX 413741 0235 ✳

Production: Lead   Ore(tons) Metal(tons)   Value(£)
            1873   2.90   2.10   36.50
            Comment 1873 INC.FORTESCUE
            Copper   Ore(tons) Metal(tons)   Value(£)
            1866   222.00   7.80   474.70
            1867   585.00   20.10   1404.90
            1868   1049.00   47.60   3028.40
            1869   1198.00   69.50   4371.60
            1870   1388.00   89.60   5472.60
            1871   1194.00   69.80   4314.40
            1872   1130.00   56.20   4221.80
            1873   797.00   42.70   2435.30
            1874   560.00   40.60   2652.60
            1875   798.00   46.90   3485.60
            1876   876.00   38.70   2479.00
            1877   795.00   37.70   1922.30
            1878   299.50   12.10   535.50
            Comment 1866-1870 (C)MARIA AND FORTESCUE; 1871-1875 (C)INC.
            FORTESCUE; 1877-1878 (C) MARIA AND FORTESCUE
            Tin   Black(tons) Stuff(tons) Tin(tons)   Value(£)
            1873   0.20   15.00
            1874   1.10   47.00
            Comment 1873-1874 INC.FORTESCUE.VALUE EST.
            Arsenic   Ore(tons) Metal(tons)   Value(£)
            1873   18.80   37.80
            1874   244.30   488.60
            1875   277.40   554.70
            1876   142.10   710.60
            1877   164.70   410.40
            1878   123.70   309.30
            Comment 1873-1878 MARIA AND FORTESCUE
Ownership: 1877-1879 WEST MARIA & FORTESCUE CONSOLS MINING CO
            Comment 1860-1873 INC.FORTESCUE; 1874-1876 WEST MARIA &
            FORTESCUE CONSOLS; 1877-1879 INC.FORTESCUE
Management: Manager 1860-1862 J.KEY; 1863-1874 WM.SKEWIS
            Chief Agent 1863-1871 JAS.DONNAL; 1872-1874 NOAH COWARD;
            1875-1876 MOSES BAWDEN & NOAH COWARD; 1877-1879 MOSES BAWDEN
            Secretary 1860-1862 JOHN BAYLY & SON (P); 1863-1868
            JAS.WATSON; 1869-1879 J.E.WATSON
Employment: Underground   Surface   Total
            1878   10   23   33
            Comment 1878 INC.FORTESCUE

MARTHA,GREAT   STOKE CLIMSLAND, CORNWALL   SX 388737 0236

Production: Copper   Ore(tons) Metal(tons)   Value(£)
            1861   1722.00   61.50   4657.00
            Comment 1861 (C)
Management: Chief Agent 1860-1863 HY.RICKARD

MARTHA,WEST   STOKE CLIMSLAND, CORNWALL   SX 372737 0237

Production: Copper   Ore(tons) Metal(tons)   Value(£)
            1863   104.00   2.50   166.40
            1864   266.00   5.30   301.50
            Comment 1863-1864 (C)

* MARY EMMA   LYDFORD   SX 533852 0238 *

Production: Tin No detailed return
Ownership: Comment 1862-1864 SUSPENDED
Management: Manager 1865-1866 WM.SKEWIS
            Chief Agent 1859-1861 WM.DOBLE; 1865-1866 JAS.DONNAL
            Secretary 1859-1866 JOS.MATTHEWS (P)

MARY GREAT CONSOLS   ST.NEOT   SX 187672 0239

Production: Copper   Ore(tons) Metal(tons)   Value(£)
            1854   396.00   22.20   2044.20
            1855   244.00   17.30   1730.70
            1856   333.00   25.40   2382.10
            1858   272.00   20.70   1856.00
            1859   313.00   22.00   2087.80
            1860   377.00   26.90   2299.30
            1861   162.00   10.70   863.20
            1862   7.00   0.20   11.20
            1864   7.00   0.10   9.10
            Comment 1854-1856 (C); 1858-1859 (C); 1860-1862 (C) CORNWALL;
            1864 (C) CORNWALL

MARY HUTCHINGS   PLYMPTON   SX 565581 0240

Production: Tin   Black(tons) Stuff(tons)   Tin(tons)   Value(£)
            1866   19.60   964.80
            1867   42.70   2348.10
            1868   49.70   2873.60
            1869   62.00   4598.60
            1870   42.60   3265.60
            1871   68.50   5720.00
            1872   63.50   5807.80
            1873   30.90   2479.60
            1874   22.10   1310.40
            1875   16.80   899.60
            1876   4.10   183.00

Tin	Black(tons)	Stuff(tons)	Tin(tons)	Value(£)
1877	1.60			68.80
1878	0.60			18.00
1879	0.50			13.70
1880	1.80			78.30

Comment 1867 MARY HUTCHINS; 1873 MARY HUTCHENS

Arsenic	Ore(tons)	Metal(tons)	Value(£)
1873	72.00		87.10
1874	5.30		9.30
1876	7.00		14.40
1878	172.20		778.40
1879	6.60		23.00

Arsenic Pyrite	Ore(tons)	Value(£)
1874	25.50	20.40
1875	70.00	56.00
1876	92.80	73.50

Comment 1876 ARSENICAL MUNDIC

Ownership: 1876-1879 WHEAL MARY HUTCHINGS MINING CO.LTD.; 1880-1881 PLYMPTON MINING & ARSENICAL CO.LTD.; 1882 MARY HUTCHINGS LTD.
Comment 1880-1881 NOW PLYMPTON MINING & ARSENIC WORKS

Management: Manager 1871-1880 HY.MINERS; 1881 PHILLIPS SLEEMAN
Chief Agent 1869 WM.EDWARDS; 1870 J.MINERS; 1874-1881 JOHN FARLEY; 1882 PHILLIPS SLEEMAN
Secretary 1869-1870 J.W.STEPHENS; 1871-1872 ALF.BROAD; 1873-1879 THOS.HORSWILL; 1880-1881 J.V.YOUNG

Employment:	Underground	Surface	Total
1878	16	18	34
1879		8	8
1880	4	4	8
1881	2		2

MARYTAVY   MARYTAVY   0241

Production: Copper No detailed return

Tin	Black(tons)	Stuff(tons)	Tin(tons)	Value(£)
1852	No detailed return			

Comment 1852 SEE PETERTAVY
Ownership: Comment 1860-1865 SEE PETERTAVY

MERRIPITT,LOWER   POSTBRIDGE   0242

Production:
Tin	Black(tons)	Stuff(tons)	Tin(tons)	Value(£)
1888	0.40			24.00
1889	0.50			24.00

Ownership: 1888 ED.MOGRIDGE
Comment 1888 LOWER MERRYPIT
Management: Chief Agent 1888 JOHN WEBB

Employment:	Underground	Surface	Total
1888	8	4	12

Production:

Copper	Ore(tons)	Metal(tons)	Value(£)
1878	22.00	2.20	119.40
1880	78.00	8.00	459.30
1881	40.00	4.50	269.40
1882	115.40	11.80	808.00
1883	67.60	3.30	200.00
1884	97.00		380.00
1885	69.00		272.00
1886	219.00		697.00
1887	66.00		312.00
1888	283.00		1429.00
1889	439.00		1209.00
1890	237.00		624.00
1891	100.00		210.00

Comment 1878 FORMERLY BELSTONE; 1880 (S)(I) FORMERLY
BELSTONE; 1881 FORMERLY BELSTONE

Arsenic Pyrite	Ore(tons)	Value(£)
1887	19.00	17.00
1889	20.00	10.00
1891	19.00	23.00

Ownership: 1880-1882 MID-DEVON COPPER MINING CO.; 1887-1890 MID-DEVON
COPPER MINING CO.; 1891 MID-DEVON COPPER MINING CO.LTD.
Comment 1878-1879 SEE BELSTONE; 1880-1882 FORMERLY BELSTONE;
1887-1890 FORMERLY BELSTONE; 1891 ABANDONED

Management: Manager 1880-1882 JAS.NEILL
Chief Agent 1887-1891 JAS.NEILL

Employment:

	Underground	Surface	Total
1878	6	7	13
1879	22	10	32
1880	26	11	37
1881	8	8	16
1882	13	10	23
1883	12	13	25
1887	9	8	17
1888	23	20	43
1889	17	23	40
1890	18	19	37
1891	5	9	14

MOLLAND   MOLLAND   SS 818283 0244

Production:

Copper	Ore(tons)	Metal(tons)	Value(£)
1845	134.00		
1846	3.00		
1852	100.00	6.70	627.80
1853	105.00	6.80	723.00
1854	85.00	6.10	625.70
1855	83.00	6.10	648.30
1856	48.00	3.10	275.20
1857	123.00	6.90	717.60
1860	180.00	11.90	1095.00
1861	120.00	7.20	628.50

MOLLAND   MOLLAND   Continued

Copper	Ore(tons)	Metal(tons)	Value(£)
1862	209.00	13.20	1126.20
1863	205.00	14.00	1136.10
1864	155.00	9.30	815.70
1865	78.00	4.60	398.40
1866	75.00	5.50	386.60
1867	55.00	2.70	188.90

Comment 1845-1846 (S); 1852-1857 (S); 1860-1867 (C)

Iron	Ore(tons)	Iron(%)	Value(£)
1877	200.00		100.00
1878	500.00		250.00
1879	387.70		193.80
1880	1681.50		1008.60
1881	230.00		80.50
1884	1226.00		307.00
1885	1608.00		402.00
1886	978.00		245.00
1890	4125.00		1031.00
1891	4330.00	49.00	1082.00
1892	2472.00		618.00
1893	No detailed return		

Comment 1877-1881 BH.; 1884-1886 BH.; 1890-1893 BH.
Ownership: 1877-1881 MOLLAND MINING CO.; 1883-1891 MOLLAND MINING CO.
Management: Chief Agent 1859-1867 THOS.BENNETT; 1877-1880 HY.BOYNS; 1881
            JOHN BOYNS; 1883-1888 JOS.POPE; 1889-1890 JOHN BRAYLEY
            Secretary 1859-1861 THOS.BENNETT (P); 1862-1867 W.NICHOLSON
Employment:

	Underground	Surface	Total
1879		6	6
1880			
1883	12	2	14
1884-1885	6	2	8
1886	5	3	8
1887	11	2	13
1889-1890	22	8	30

Comment 1880 SEE BRIMLEY

MOLTON CONSOLS,SOUTH   SOUTH MOLTON   SS 701285 0245

Production: Lead & Silver

	Ore(tons)	Lead(tons)	Silver(ozs)	Value(£)
1850	60.00	46.00		
1851-1854	No detailed return			
1875	5.20	4.40	24.00	
1878	14.60	9.50	40.00	130.20

Copper	Ore(tons)	Metal(tons)	Value(£)
1846	2.00		

Comment 1846 (S) SOUTH MOLTON
Ownership: 1877-1880 SOUTH MOLTON CONSOLS MINING CO.
            Comment 1875-1876 SOUTH MOLTON; 1880 NOT WORKED
Management: Chief Agent 1875-1876 A.S.LORDOCK; 1877 ZACH.JAMES; 1878
            W.H.WATSON & THOS.MAY
            Secretary 1878-1880 W.H.WATSON (S)

MOLTON CONSOLS,SOUTH   SOUTH MOLTON   Continued

Employment: Underground   Surface   Total
                    1878   8   5   13
                    1879   6   6

MOLTON,NORTH   NORTH MOLTON   0246

Production: Copper   Ore(tons) Metal(tons)   Value(£)
                    1845   4.00
                    1846   5.00
            Comment 1845-1846 (S)

✳ MONKSTON   BRENTOR   SX 469809 0247 ✳

Production: Manganese   Ore(tons) Metal(tons)   Value(£)
                    1879   57.00   85.00
                    1880   720.00   1260.00
                    1882   80.00   275.00
                    1883   308.00   760.00
                    1884   No detailed return
                    1885   1150.00
                    1886   855.00   2166.00
                    1887   95.00   112.00
                    1888   No detailed return
            Comment 1879-1880 MONKSTONE
Ownership: 1879-1887 W.R.HAWARD
Management: Manager 1873 JOHN GOLDSWORTHY
            Chief Agent 1874-1878 JAS.DUNSMORE; 1879-1883 JOHN
            GOLDSWORTHY; 1884-1887 JOHN VARCOE
            Secretary 1873-1879 WILKIN & CLARKE
Employment: Underground   Surface   Total
                    1879   10   18   28
                    1880   29   17   46
                    1881   18   7   25
                    1882   15   14   29
                    1883   16   14   30
                    1884   6   10   16
                    1885   40   26   66
                    1886   60   45   105

NAPDOWN   COMBE MARTIN   SS 597466 0248

✳ NARRACOTT   MILTON ABBOT   0249 ✳

Production: Manganese   Ore(tons) Metal(tons)   Value(£)
                    1873   153.00   832.30
                    1874   115.00   517.00
                    1875   68.00   408.00
Ownership: Comment 1875 IN LIQUIDATION

86

NARRACOTT   MILTON ABBOT   Continued

Management: Chief Agent 1873-1874 JNO.GOLDSWORTHY
     Secretary 1872-1875 G.B.SANDEMAN

NEW CONSOLS   STOKE CLIMSLAND, CORNWALL SX 388737 0250

Production: Copper   Ore(tons) Metal(tons) Value(£)
    1874   No detailed return
    Comment 1874 SEE EMMENS UNITED MINES

NEW GREAT CONSOLS   STOKE CLIMSLAND, CORNWALL SX 388737 0251

Production: Copper No detailed return
Management: Manager 1868-1870 R.PRYOR
    Chief Agent 1868-1869 R.TRATHAN; 1870
    THOS.BENNETT,H.TREGONNING & R.TRATHAN

NEWTON MINING COMPANY   NEWTON ST CYRES   SX 876965 0252

Management: Manager 1859 J.HARRIS

NEWTON ST. CYRES   NEWTON ST. CYRES   SX 880973 0253

Production: Manganese   Ore(tons) Metal(tons) Value(£)
    1873   191.40   1288.00
    1874   304.00   2018.00
    1875   109.20   545.00
    1876   129.00   600.00
    1877   287.30   574.00
    1878   200.00   400.00
    1879   40.00   40.00
    Comment 1873-1878 NEWTON ST.CYRUS
Ownership: 1877-1881 SIMS BROS.
Management: Manager 1872 WM.YEW; 1873-1875 WM.DOIDGE; 1876-1881 HY.SIMS
    Chief Agent 1876-1881 WM.DOIDGE
    Secretary 1873-1876 SIMS BROS.
Employment: Underground Surface   Total
    1878   2   3   5
    1879   2   5   7

NOEMIA   SHAUGH   SX 535638 0254

Production: Iron   Ore(tons) Iron(%) Value(£)
    1875   175.00   131.50
    1876   222.00   111.00
    1881   250.00   125.00
    Comment 1875 BH.; 1876 BH.5TONS TRIED FOR BRICKMAKING; 1881
    BH.
Ownership: 1875-1876 LEWIS & CASPER; 1877 LEWIS & CO.; 1881 FERRO

CERAMIC CO.LTD.
Comment 1876-1877 NOEMIE; 1881 NOEMIE
Management: Chief Agent 1875-1876 RICH.STEVENS; 1877 G.COOK; 1881 JOHN
CANNING
Employment: Underground   Surface   Total
            1881   8   8   16

✳ NUNS CROSS   WALKHAMPTON   SX 602699 0255

Production: Tin No detailed return
Ownership: Comment 1865 SUSPENDED
Management: Manager 1862 JOHN GIFFORD
            Chief Agent 1862-1864 THOS.FOOT
            Secretary 1862-1865 THOS.HORSWILL

✳ OKEHAMPTON   OKEHAMPTON   0256

Production: Copper No detailed return
Management: Manager 1866-1867 JOS.RICHARDS

OLDERTOWN   ILSINGTON   0258

Production: Iron No detailed return
Ownership: 1873-1875 WM.BROWNE
Management: Chief Agent 1873-1875 WM.GROSE

OWLACOMBE   ASHBURTON   SX 771733 0259

Production: Copper   Ore(tons) Metal(tons)   Value(£)
            1909   No detailed return
            Comment 1909 SEE STORMSDOWN
            Tin   Black(tons) Stuff(tons) Tin(tons)   Value(£)
            1854   0.70   50.90
            1887   5.00   250.00
            1888   2.00   100.00
            1889   0.50   27.00
            1890   0.50   25.00
            1892   0.30   16.00
            1907-1909 No detailed return
            1912-1913 No detailed return
            Comment 1887 OLD OWLACOMBE; 1892 OLD OWLACOMBE; 1907-1909 SEE
            STORMSDOWN; 1912-1913 SEE STORMSDOWN
            Arsenic   Ore(tons) Metal(tons)   Value(£)
            1887   50.00   300.00
            1888   12.00   72.00
            1892   2.00   8.00
            1913   No detailed return
            Comment 1887 OLD OWLACOMBE; 1913 SEE STORMSDOWN

Arsenic Pyrite	Ore(tons)	Value(£)
1881	50.00	37.50
1885	150.00	150.00
1886	500.00	500.00

Comment 1885-1886 ORE UNDRESSED INC 2% TIN

Ownership: 1881-1883 OLD OWLACOMBE MINING CO.LTD.; 1885-1887 H.HEWITT; 1888 FLEM.HEWITT; 1889-1893 EDW.TUCKER

Comment 1881 OLD OWLACOMBE FORMERLY WEST BEAM; 1882 OLD OWLACOMBE; 1883 OLD OWLACOMBE NOT WORKED IN 1883; 1885-1889 OLD OWLACOMBE; 1890-1891 OLD OWLACOMBE SUSPENDED; 1892 OLD OWLACOMBE; 1893 OLD OWLACOMBE ABANDONED; 1907-1913 SEE STORMSDOWN

Management: Manager 1881 GEO.MUDGE
Chief Agent 1882-1883 W.H.HOSKING; 1887-1893 GEO.MUDGE
Secretary 1881 H.A.MORRIS; 1885-1886 H.A.MORRIS

Employment:

	Underground	Surface	Total
1881	6	2	8
1882	6	3	9
1885	8	4	12
1886	4	9	13
1888		3	3
1889-1890		4	4
1892	4		4
1907-1913			

Comment 1907-1913 SEE STORMSDOWN

 PARK   BERE ALSTON   0260

Production:

Lead & Silver	Ore(tons)	Lead(tons)	Silver(ozs)	Value(£)
1855	45.00	35.00		
1856	160.00	123.00		
1857	205.00	157.70	50.00	

Comment 1856 FOR AG SEE CARPENTER

 PARK VALLEY   SPREYTON   SX 713990 0261

Production: Lead & Silver No detailed return
Ownership: 1878-1883 PARK VALLEY MINING CO.LTD.
Comment 1880-1882 NOT WORKED; 1883 NOT WORKED IN 1883
Management: Manager 1878-1881 W.H.HOSKING
Chief Agent 1879-1881 EDW.DIPSTALE; 1882-1883 W.H.HOSKING
Employment:

	Underground	Surface	Total
1879	4		4

PARKINS   BRIXHAM   0262

Production:

Iron	Ore(tons)	Iron(%)	Value(£)
1870	650.00		195.00
1871	1000.00		750.00

Comment 1870-1871 BH.PARKERS MINE

89

Ownership: 1869-1873 WM.BROWNE
              Comment 1870-1872 PARKIN; 1873 PARKERS
Management: Chief Agent 1869-1873 PHAR.GROSE

PARRACOMBE   PARRACOMBE   SS 665453 0263

Production: Lead & Silver No detailed return
Ownership: 1877 CHAS.H.MAUNDER & OTHERS; 1878-1880 PARRACOMBE MINING
              CO.
              Comment 1877 SEE PARRACOMBE, SOMERSET; 1880 NOT WORKED
Management: Chief Agent 1877 CHAS.H.MAUNDER
              Secretary 1878-1880 F.E.YOUNG
Employment: Underground   Surface   Total
              1878   4   4

PAWTON   ST.BREOCK, CORNWALL   SW 952701 0264

Production: Iron No detailed return
Ownership: 1871 WELSH IRON WORKS
Management: Chief Agent 1871 W.H.HOSKING

PETERTAVY   MARYTAVY   0265

Production: Copper No detailed return
             Tin   Black(tons) Stuff(tons)   Tin(tons)   Value(£)
             1852   1.10
             Comment 1852 TETERTAVY & MARYTAVY
Ownership: Comment 1860-1861 INC.MARYTAVY; 1862-1865 INC.MARYTAVY
             SUSPENDED
Management: Manager 1860-1861 JOHN LEAN
             Secretary 1860-1865 JOHN LEAN (P)

PLAISTOW   SHIRWELL   SS 567387 0266

Production: Iron   Ore(tons)   Iron(%)   Value(£)
             1874   240.00   240.00
             Comment 1874 BH.

PLUMLEY   BOVEY TRACEY   SX 804806 0267

Production: Iron   Ore(tons)   Iron(%)   Value(£)
             1896-1897 No detailed return
             1898   54.00
             1899   50.00
             1900   50.00
             1901   75.00
             1902   15.00
             1903   3.00

Iron	Ore(tons)	Iron(%)	Value(£)
1904	60.00		
1905	75.00		
1906	60.00		
1907	50.00		
1908	80.00		
1909	47.00		
1910	50.00		
1911	26.00		

Comment 1896-1897 SEE HAWKMOOR; 1898-1901 MH.; 1902-1911
MICACEOUS HAEMATITE,RETURNED AS UMBER

Ownership: 1896-1899 P.J.DICK; 1900-1901 JAS.DICK; 1902-1906 TRUSTEES OF
THE LATE JAS.DICK; 1907-1913 FERRUBRON MANUFACTURING CO.
Comment 1903-1909 SUSPENDED; 1911 SUSPENDED AUG.1911; 1912
NOT WORKED; 1913 NOT WORKED SHUTDOWN

Management: Chief Agent 1896-1902 A.LIVINGSTONE; 1909-1913 W.H.HOSKING
Secretary 1907-1913 W.H.HOSKING

Employment:

	Underground	Surface	Total
1896	2	4	6
1897	2	5	7
1898	4	4	8
1900	4	5	9
1901	9		9
1902	2	2	4
1903	1		1
1904	2	2	4
1905	4	2	6
1906	3	1	4
1907	4	1	5
1908-1909	3	1	4
1910	4	1	5
1911	2	1	3

PLYMPTON MINING ARSENIC WORKS   PLYMPTON   SX 565581 0268

Production: Tin No detailed return
Ownership: Comment 1880-1881 SEE MARY HUTCHINGS

POLHARMAN   TYWARDREATH, CORNWALL   SX 084567 0269

Production: Copper	Ore(tons)	Metal(tons)	Value(£)
1865	101.00	5.40	417.60
1866	73.00	4.20	279.40
1867	118.00	7.10	462.20

Comment 1865-1867 (C)

POLTIMORE   NORTH MOLTON   SS 699322 0270

Production: Copper	Ore(tons)	Metal(tons)	Value(£)
1854	13.00		

                Comment 1854 (S)
                Iron No detailed return
Ownership: 1873-1878 ALL.GRANGER
Management: Chief Agent 1873-1878 HOLM.GRANGER

PORTLEMOUTH CONSOLS   EAST PORTLEMOUTH   SX 758389 0271

Production: Iron   Ore(tons)   Iron(%)   Value(£)
            1859   1921.80   672.00
            1860   No detailed return
            Comment 1859 HE.INC S.DEVON PRAWLE&DICTORS; 1860
            HE.ISLAND.LISTED AS HANTS 1866
Ownership: Comment 1865 SUSPENDED
Management: Chief Agent 1860-1864 R.EDMONDS
            Secretary 1860-1865 H.H.DOCKER (P)

PRAWLE   PRAWLE POINT   SX 772353 0272

Production: Iron   Ore(tons)   Iron(%)   Value(£)
            1858   300.00   142.50
            1859-1861 No detailed return
            Comment 1858 BH.; 1859 BH.SEE PORTLEMOUTH CONSOLS; 1860-1861
            BH.
Ownership: Comment 1863-1866 SUSPENDED
Management: Chief Agent 1867-1868 CAPT.DENNIS

* PRINCE ARTHUR CONSOLS   MARYTAVY   SX 510812 0273

Production: Lead & Silver   Ore(tons) Lead(tons) Silver(ozs)   Value(£)
            1865   21.00   15.00   176.00
            1866   208.00   149.00   1872.00
            1867   233.70   175.30   2679.00
            Comment 1865-1866 PRINCE ARTHUR
Ownership: Comment 1863 PRINCE ALFRED CONSOLS OR OLD BETSY; 1864-1871 OR
            OLD BETSY
Management: Manager 1864-1866 JAS.RICHARDS; 1867-1871 WM.GEORGE
            Chief Agent 1863-1866 WM.GEORGE
            Secretary 1863 JAS.RICHARDS; 1864-1867 JNO.THOMSON; 1868-1871
            T.CURRIE GREGORY

PRINCE OF WALES   CALSTOCK, CORNWALL   SX 401705 0274

Ownership: 1879 PRINCE OF WALES MINING CO.
Management: Chief Agent 1879 JNO.ANDREWS

PROSPER   BRIXHAM   0275

Production: Iron   Ore(tons)   Iron(%)   Value(£)
            1872   1415.00   849.00
            1873   768.00   576.00
            1874   503.00   278.00
            Comment 1872-1874 BH.
Ownership: 1864-1872 R.W.WOLSTON; 1873-1874 J.R.RENDALL
Management: Chief Agent 1864-1872 CAPT.DENNIS; 1873 JOHN BOVEY; 1874
            SML.LAKE

QUEEN OF DART   BUCKFASTLEIGH   SX 734688 0276

Production: Copper   Ore(tons) Metal(tons)   Value(£)
            1854   47.00
            1855   124.00   7.10   435.20
            1856   253.00   11.80   934.30
            1857   234.00   8.30   786.60
            Comment 1854 (S) DART MINE; 1855 (S); 1856 (C)(S); 1857 (S)
Ownership: Comment 1863-1865 SUSPENDED

QUEEN OF TAMAR   BEER FERRIS   SX 450674 0277

Production: Lead No detailed return
            Copper No detailed return
Ownership: Comment 1862-1865 SUSPENDED
Management: Manager 1860-1861 C.WILLIAMS
            Chief Agent 1860-1861 B.ROBBINS
            Secretary 1860-1865 C.WILLIAMS (P)

RAMSDOWN   MILTON ABBOT   SX 414808 0278

Production: Manganese   Ore(tons) Metal(tons)   Value(£)
            1880   No detailed return
            Comment 1880 DEVON MANGANESE MINING CO.
Ownership: 1878-1881 GEO.SEYMOUR
Management: Chief Agent 1878-1881 GEO.SEYMOUR
            Secretary 1878-1881 JACOB LEGASSICK
Employment: Underground   Surface   Total
            1878   18   8   26

RAMSLEY   STICKLEPATH   SX 650930 0279

Production: Copper   Ore(tons) Metal(tons)   Value(£)
            1902   69.00   224.00
            1904   210.00   23.00   1010.00
            1905   815.00   4818.00
            1906   910.00   6732.00
            1907   652.00   4103.00
            1908   664.00   57.00   1919.00
            1909   432.00   1956.00

                                    93

Ownership: 1899-1911 RAMSLEY EXPLORATION SYNDICATE
             Comment 1860-1866 RAMSLEY HILL; 1899-1904 OR EMILY; 1905-1909
             FORMERLY EMILY & BELSTONE; 1910-1911 EMILY & BELSTONE IN
             LIQUIDATION
Management: Manager 1860-1866 JAS.HAMPTON
             Chief Agent 1860-1866 JOHN DAW; 1899-1900 A.L.BEGBIE;
             1901-1905 D.S.WARNE; 1906-1911 CHAS.E.JOBLING
             Secretary 1860-1866 JAS.HAMPTON (P)

Employment:	Underground	Surface	Total
1900	7	26	33
1901	19	12	31
1902	19	9	28
1903	16	7	23
1904	38	24	62
1905	54	43	97
1906	56	32	88
1907	47	42	89
1908	50	44	94
1909	20	25	45
1910	2	2	4
1911		4	4

RAVEN ROCK   TAVISTOCK   SX 471694 0280

Production: Tin	Black(tons)	Stuff(tons)	Tin(tons)	Value(£)
1858	4.10			259.90

RICHARDS FRIENDSHIP   ST.HILARY, CORNWALL   0281

Production: Copper	Ore(tons)	Metal(tons)	Value(£)
1854	104.00	6.30	627.20
1855	252.00	13.60	1312.90

Comment 1854-1855 (C)

RILEY   HENNOCK   SX 844800 0282

Production: Manganese	Ore(tons)	Metal(tons)	Value(£)
1875	118.00		590.00

Ownership: 1877 J.BROWN & SON
Management: Chief Agent 1874 W.GROVE; 1875-1877 JAS.MOUNSTEPHEN
             Secretary 1875-1876 J.BROWN & SON

RIX HILL   TAVISTOCK   SX 482723 0283

Production: Tin	Black(tons)	Stuff(tons)	Tin(tons)	Value(£)
1852	60.60			
1853	54.40			3402.60
1854	11.00			634.10
1855	8.50			432.70

Comment 1852 TIN ORE

★ ROBERT,NORTH   SAMPFORD SPINEY   SX 513708 0284 ★

Production:	Lead	Ore(tons)	Metal(tons)	Value(£)	
	1866	1.80	1.20		
	Copper	Ore(tons)	Metal(tons)	Value(£)	
	1853	208.00	19.20	1834.00	
	1854	408.00	28.20	2782.90	
	1855	590.00	45.60	4685.40	
	1856	1220.00	86.60	8955.60	
	1857	1345.00	94.40	2371.00	
	1858	1109.00	81.50	7522.30	
	1859	1414.00	104.30	9752.90	
	1860	1090.00	89.90	8425.70	
	1861	961.00	75.90	6632.30	
	1862	1154.00	96.30	7692.00	
	1863	514.00	26.30	1852.80	
	1864	331.00	19.90	1615.90	
	1865	312.00	20.10	1588.90	
	1866	76.00	4.30	266.40	
	Comment 1853-1866 (C)				
	Tin	Black(tons)	Stuff(tons)	Tin(tons)	Value(£)
	1864	42.00			2599.20
	1865	25.50			1381.40
	1866	16.80			860.40

Ownership: Comment 1866-1867 VERY GREATLY REDUCED
Management: Manager 1859-1863 JAS.RICHARDS
            Chief Agent 1859-1867 W.GODDEN
            Secretary 1859-1867 JOS.MATTHEWS (P)

★ ROBERT,SOUTH   HORRABRIDGE   0285 ★

Production:	Tin	Black(tons)	Stuff(tons)	Tin(tons)	Value(£)
	1863	23.10			1537.50

★ ROBOROUGH DOWN   BUCKLAND MONACHORUM   0287 ★

Ownership: Comment 1865 SUSPENDED
Management: Chief Agent 1864 THOS.FOOT
            Secretary 1864-1865 GEO.DOWN

ROCK HILL   ILSINGTON   0288

Production: Iron No detailed return
Ownership: 1873 WM.BROWNE
Management: Manager 1873 WM.GROSE

Management: Chief Agent 1878-1881 T.S.HOSKING
            Secretary 1878-1881 CHAS.H.MAUNDER
            Comment 1878-1881 COULD BE GREAT RODD, CORNWALL

✳ RUSSELL   TAVISTOCK   SX 438711 0290✳

Production: Copper   Ore(tons) Metal(tons)   Value(£)
            1852   181.00   10.20   763.40
            1853   167.00   10.00   938.80
            1854   471.00   24.40   2362.90
            1855   584.00   28.50   2827.10
            1856   363.00   22.30   2081.70
            1857   254.00   10.40   918.00
            1858   282.00   10.50   909.50
            1868   171.00   11.40   800.50
            1869   247.00   11.20   661.10
            1870   534.00   36.60   2179.70
            1871   1055.00   69.10   4329.00
            1872   974.00   42.40   3067.40
            1873   598.00   37.10   2209.20
            1874   1191.00   64.90   4153.90
            1875   1152.00   51.80   3816.60
            1876   1119.00   44.80   2789.20
            1877   387.10   13.20   719.10
            1878   60.00   2.20   94.20
            1881   72.70   3.50   163.60
            1885   71.00   149.00
            1886   69.00   53.00
            1888   28.00   108.00
            1891   8.00   30.00
            Comment 1852-1854 (C) RUSSEL; 1855-1858 (C); 1868-1876 (C);
            1877 RUSSEL; 1881 RUSSELL UNITED; 1885-1886 RUSSELL UNITED;
            1888 RUSSELL UNITED; 1891 RUSSELL MINES
            Tin   Black(tons) Stuff(tons)   Tin(tons)   Value(£)
            1885   4.00   74.00   197.00
            1886   2.50   43.70   109.00
            1887-1888 No detailed return
            1889   0.10   9.00   6.00
            1891   4.50   240.00
            1892   8.00   29.00
            Comment 1885-1888 RUSSELL UNITED
            Arsenic Pyrite Ore(tons)   Value(£)
            1891   10.00   11.00
            Comment 1891 RUSSELL MINES
Ownership: 1877-1879 WHEAL RUSSELL MINING CO.; 1880-1886 WHEAL RUSSELL
            UNITED MINING CO.; 1887-1888 WHEAL RUSSELL UNITED MINING
            CO.LTD.; 1889-1893 RUSSELL MINES CO.LTD.
            Comment 1881-1888 RUSSELL UNITED; 1893 ABANDONED
Management: Chief Agent 1859 JAS.BRAY; 1861-1877 JAS.BRAY; 1878-1888 JOHN
            BRAY; 1889-1893 WM.GEORGE
            Secretary 1859 JOS.MATTHEWS (P); 1861-1877 JOS.MATTHEWS (P);
            1880 M.GREENFIELD (P); 1881 J.W.GREENFIELD (S); 1891-1893

ED.ASHMEAD (S)

Employment:	Underground	Surface	Total
1878	12	10	22
1879	12	2	14
1880	27	9	36
1881	30	10	40
1882	26	4	30
1883	22	6	28
1884	16	6	22
1885	23	21	44
1886	30	12	42
1888	13	6	19
1889	29	15	44
1890	30	17	47
1891	18	8	26
1892	19	7	26
1893	1	2	3

RUSSELL,EAST   TAVISTOCK   SX 450710 0291

Production: Copper	Ore(tons)	Metal(tons)	Value(£)
1853	60.00	5.60	524.50
1857	132.00	9.30	883.20
1858	330.00	31.70	2983.00
1859	419.00	33.60	3214.80
1860	1101.00	97.40	8994.70
1861	1416.00	95.60	8198.40
1862	1224.00	79.80	6270.70
1863	1262.00	77.40	5670.30
1864	1123.00	67.20	5589.20
1865	840.00	45.10	3377.00
1866	892.00	56.80	3768.40
1867	583.00	35.30	2364.80
1868	518.00	30.50	1885.80
1869	50.00	2.90	182.80

Comment 1853 (C); 1857-1869 (C)
Management: Manager 1859-1866 JAS.RICHARDS; 1867 WM.RICHARDS
Chief Agent 1859-1866 JOHN GOLDSWORTHY
Secretary 1859-1866 W.E.CUMMINS (P); 1867 WM.RICHARDS

RUSSELL,NEW EAST   TAVISTOCK   SX 465714 0292

Production: Copper	Ore(tons)	Metal(tons)	Value(£)
1863	27.00	1.50	100.60
1865	47.00	2.80	214.90
1866	68.00	5.60	373.60
1867	86.00	7.40	534.10
1868	84.00	6.60	446.60

Comment 1863 (C); 1865-1868 (C)
Management: Chief Agent 1861-1862 THOS.BAWDEN; 1863-1867 JNO.GIFFORD;
1869 JNO.GIFFORD

Secretary 1861-1867 H.E.CROKER (P); 1869 JOHN HITCHINS

SALCOMBE   SALCOMBE   0293

Production: Iron	Ore(tons)	Iron(%)	Value(£)
1872	100.00		60.00

Comment 1872 HE.
Ownership: 1870-1872 VAN IRON ORE CO.
Management: Chief Agent 1870-1872 W.H.HOSKING

SHAPTOR   BOVEY TRACEY   SX 806810 0294

Production: Iron	Ore(tons)	Iron(%)	Value(£)
1894-1897 No detailed return			
1898	74.00		
1899	90.00		
1900	88.00		
1901	90.00		
1902	20.00		
1903	40.00		
1904	40.00		
1905	60.00		
1906	74.00		
1907	60.00		
1908	55.00		
1909	51.00		
1910	20.00		
1911	53.00		

Comment 1894-1897 MH.SHAPTER SEE HAWKMOOR; 1898-1901
MH.INC.SHUTTAMOOR; 1902-1911 MICACEOUS HAEMATITE,RETURNED AS
UMBER
Ownership: 1892 NELSON BIRD; 1893-1901 G.M.SLATTER; 1902-1913 FERRUBRON
MANUFACTURING CO.
Comment 1897-1910 INC.SHUTTAMOOR; 1911 INC.SHUTTAMOOR
SUSPENDED AUG.1911; 1912 INC.SHUTTAMOOR NOT WORKED; 1913
INC.SHUTTAMOOR NOT WORKED SHUTDOWN
Management: Chief Agent 1909-1913 W.H.HOSKING
Secretary 1903-1913 W.H.HOSKING

Employment:	Underground	Surface	Total
1892	1	1	2
1893	5	3	8
1894	12	6	18
1895	9	5	14
1896	7	5	12
1897	6	4	10
1898	4	2	6
1900		7	7
1901	8	2	10
1902	2	1	3
1903	2	2	4
1904	3	1	4

	Underground	Surface	Total
1905	4	1	5
1906-1907	4	2	6
1908	4	1	5
1909	4	2	6
1911-1913	2	1	3

Comment 1897-1898 INC.SHUTTAMOOR; 1900-1909 INC.SHUTTAMOOR;
1911-1913 INC.SHUTTAMOOR

SHARKHAM   BRIXHAM   SX 934547 0295

Production: Iron	Ore(tons)	Iron(%)	Value(£)
1860-1862 No detailed return			
1865	14928.00		5038.00
1866	560.00		
1868	3425.00		1027.50
1871-1872 No detailed return			

Comment 1860-1861 BH.SHARKHAM POINT SEE BRIXHAM; 1862
BH.SHARHAM POINT SEE BRIXHAM; 1865 BH.INC.CHINTER & FIVE
ACRES; 1866 BH.FOR VALUE SEE DREWS; 1868 BH.; 1871
BH.SHARKHAM PT.SEE TORBAY IRON; 1872 BH.SHARKAM SEE TORBAY
IRON
Ownership: 1864-1871 WM.BROWNE
Comment 1864-1871 SHARPHAM; 1872-1874 SEE TORBAY IRON
Management: Chief Agent 1864 WM.GROSE; 1865-1871 PHAR.GROSE

SHAUGH   SHAUGH PRIOR   SX 533633 0296

Production: Iron	Ore(tons)	Iron(%)	Value(£)
1870	1307.00		590.00
1871	No detailed return		
1872	1591.00		403.90
1873	807.40		625.90
1874	965.00		723.50

Comment 1870 BH.; 1871 BH.EXPLORING FOR LEAD & COPPER;
1872-1874 BH.
Ownership: 1869-1876 JOHN BROGDEN & SON
Management: Chief Agent 1869-1872 H.GORDON; 1873-1876 JOHN J.PEACOCK

SHIRWELL   PLAISTOW   SS 606383 0297

Production: Manganese	Ore(tons)	Metal(tons)	Value(£)
1873	5.00		20.00

Comment 1873 INC.BRATTON FLEMING

Iron	Ore(tons)	Iron(%)	Value(£)
1873	40.00		40.00
1874	250.00		200.00

Comment 1873 BH.SHEWELL INC.BRATTON FLEMING; 1874
BH.SHIRWELLINC.BRATTON FLEMING
Ownership: 1873-1874 SIR A.CHICHESTER; 1875-1877 R.DAWSON CLEGG

SHIRWELL	PLAISTOW	Continued

Comment 1873-1878 INC.BRATTON FLEMING
Management: Manager 1873-1878 T.TRESIDER
Chief Agent 1873-1878 T.PLINT
Secretary 1873-1878 R.DAWSON CLEGG

SHIRWELL FORD	SHIRWELL	SS 599378 0298

Production:
Iron	Ore(tons)	Iron(%)	Value(£)
1874	5.00		5.00

Comment 1874 BH.

SHOTTS	ILSINGTON	SX 773773 0299

Production: Iron No detailed return
Ownership: 1873 WM.BROWNE
Management: Manager 1873 WM.GROSE

SHUTTAMOOR	BOVEY TRACEY	SX 823829 0300

Production:
Iron	Ore(tons)	Iron(%)	Value(£)
1897-1911 No detailed return			

Comment 1897 SEE HAWKMOOR; 1898 SHOUTAMOOR SEE SHAPTOR;
1899-1901 SHORTAMOOR SEE SHAPTOR; 1902-1911 SEE SHAPTOR
Ownership: Comment 1897-1905 SHORTAMOOR SEE SHAPTOR; 1906-1913
SHOOTAMOOR SEE SHAPTOR
Employment:
	Underground	Surface	Total
1897-1898			
1900-1909			
1911-1913			

Comment 1897-1898 SEE SHAPTOR; 1900-1909 SEE SHAPTOR;
1911-1913 SEE SHAPTOR

SIDNEY	PLYMPTON	SX 551594 0301

Production:
Tin	Black(tons)	Stuff(tons)	Tin(tons)	Value(£)
1852	19.90			
1853	61.00			3878.50
1854	32.20			2262.00
1855	30.20			2550.00
1856	48.00			3649.30
1857	43.10			3500.30
1859	78.00			5448.00
1861	48.90			4011.30
1862	6.70			456.20
1863	40.50			2749.40
1864	28.60			1891.10

Comment 1852 TIN ORE; 1862 ONE QUARTER ONLY
Arsenic	Ore(tons)	Metal(tons)	Value(£)
1855	11.00		

                    Comment 1855 SYDNEY WHITE ARSENIC
Ownership: Comment 1863-1864 SYDNEY; 1865 SYDNEY SUSPENDED
Management: Manager 1871-1872 HY.MINERS
                    Chief Agent 1860-1864 WM.EDWARDS; 1872 JOHN FARLEY
                    Secretary 1860-1861 H.LINDON (P); 1862-1865 H.E.CROKER;
                    1871-1872 ALF.BROAD

SIGFORD CONSOLS   ILSINGTON   SX 774750 0302

Production: Copper No detailed return
Ownership: Comment 1863-1865 SUSPENDED
Management: Chief Agent 1860-1862 W.H.HOSKING

SILVER BROOK   ILSINGTON   SX 789759 0303

Production: Lead	Ore(tons)	Metal(tons)	Value(£)
1854	23.70	15.00	
1855	44.70	28.20	
1856	23.40	16.40	

1857-1860 No detailed return
Comment 1856 FOR AG SEE CARPENTER

Zinc	Ore(tons)	Metal(tons)	Value(£)
1854	43.20		
1855	342.90		
1856	505.90		1351.00
1857	730.40		2343.80
1858	175.00		612.60

Comment 1854 SILVERBROOK

SMALLACOMBE   ILSINGTON   SX 777766 0304

Production: Iron	Ore(tons)	Iron(%)	Value(£)
1865	No detailed return		
1866	1870.00		607.70
1867	700.00		210.00
1868	73.00		36.50
1869	507.00		152.10
1870	No detailed return		
1871	352.00		264.00
1872	1775.00		1115.00
1873	1272.30		954.00
1874	2069.00		1626.50

                    Comment 1865 BH.SEE HAYTOR; 1866-1867 BH.; 1868-1869 MO.;
                    1870-1874 BH.
Ownership: 1866-1872 WM.BROWNE; 1873-1875 NATIVE IRON ORE CO.; 1880-1881
                    PAULL & CO.
                    Comment 1864-1865 SEE ATLAS IRON; 1866 INC.ATLAS IRON;
                    1870-1871 SUSPENDED
Management: Manager 1873-1875 W.H.HOSKING
                    Chief Agent 1866-1869 WM.GROSE; 1873-1881 JNO.COCK

SMALLACOMBE   ILSINGTON

Secretary 1873-1879 NETTING & PAULL

SMITHS WOOD   ASHBURTON   SX 773748 0305

Production: Tin   Black(tons) Stuff(tons)   Tin(tons)   Value(£)
            1863   6.80   448.80
Ownership: Comment 1863-1865 SUSPENDED
Management: Chief Agent 1860-1862 W.H.HOSKING

✳ SORTRIDGE CONSOLS   WHITCHURCH   SX 510708 0306 ✳

Production: Copper   Ore(tons) Metal(tons)   Value(£)
            1854   445.00   43.90   4542.10
            1855   1138.00   118.10   12422.20
            1856   1907.00   149.60   13855.70
            1857   923.00   68.60   6694.30
            1858   714.00   51.90   4691.70
            1859   307.00   18.30   1656.10
            1860   269.00   18.60   1614.90
            1861   470.00   43.00   3767.90
            1862   657.00   56.30   4451.50
            1863   257.00   20.00   1510.70
            1864   207.00   11.70   919.90
            1865   193.00   9.90   725.90
            1866   134.00   7.80   464.10
            1867   72.00   3.90   255.00
            1868   52.00   3.40   216.00
            1869   36.00   2.70   169.10
            1871   11.00   0.30   13.30
            Comment 1854-1869 (C); 1871 (C)
            Tin   Black(tons) Stuff(tons)   Tin(tons)   Value(£)
            1883   4.50   233.00
            1885   4.50   200.00
            1886   5.80   329.00
            1887   2.70   175.00
            1888   No detailed return
            1891   6.00   300.00
            1892   8.00   432.00
            1893   2.20   125.00
            Comment 1883 SORTRIDGE; 1891-1893 SORTRIDGE
Ownership: 1881-1887 SORTRIDGE COPPER MINING CO.; 1888-1889 SORTRIDGE
            TIN MINING CO.LTD.; 1891-1894 MRS.SPRY
            Comment 1862 SUSPENDED; 1866-1868 VERY GREATLY REDUCED; 1871
            SODRIDGE CONSOLS; 1881-1889 SORTRIDGE; 1891-1894 SORTRIDGE
Management: Manager 1859-1861 JAS.RICHARDS; 1864-1868 JAS.RICHARDS
            Chief Agent 1859-1861 ROBT.JACKSON; 1863-1865 I.JACKSON;
            1866-1868 ROBT.JACKSON; 1881-1884 WM.SKEWIS
            Secretary 1859-1866 W.B.HARVEY (P); 1867-1868 JAS.RICHARDS;
            1885-1887 HY.SPRY; 1888-1889 S.HEDGER
Employment: Underground   Surface   Total
            1881   22   22

102

SORTRIDGE CONSOLS   WHITCHURCH   Continued

	Underground	Surface	Total
1882	24	12	36
1883	8	2	10
1885-1886	3		3
1887	2		2
1888	4	7	11
1889	22	26	48
1891-1893	4	2	6

SORTRIDGE,WEST   WHITCHURCH   SX 496706 0307 ✳

Production: Tin	Black(tons)	Stuff(tons)	Tin(tons)	Value(£)
1855	6.00			323.50

SPECULAR IRON ORE MINE   BUCKFASTLEIGH   0308

Production: Iron No detailed return
Ownership: 1891 SPECULAR IRON ORE MINING CO.
            Comment 1891 LETTERS SENT. NO REPLY.
Management: Chief Agent 1891 W.BOWER

SPREACOMBE VALLEY   BARNSTAPLE   SS 477412 0309

Production: Iron	Ore(tons)	Iron(%)	Value(£)
1874	378.30		233.50
1875	158.20		118.60
1876	118.10		70.80
1889	125.00		31.00
1890	No detailed return		

            Comment 1874 BH.SPRAYCOMBE; 1875-1876 BH.SPREACOMBE; 1889
            BH.SPREACOMBE VALE; 1890 BH.SPREYCOMBE
Ownership: 1874 YNYSCEDWYN CO.; 1875-1877 YNYSCEDWYN IRON WORKS CO.;
            1887-1891 SPREACOMBE MINE SYNDICATE
            Comment 1874-1877 SPREACOMBE; 1890-1891 SUSPENDED
Management: Chief Agent 1874-1877 GEO.BOYLES; 1887-1888 W.S.MINSHALL;
            1891 G.P.JAY
            Secretary 1889-1891 G.P.JAY

Employment:		Underground	Surface	Total
	1889	6	3	9

STANCOMBE   ILSINGTON   SX 801740 0310

Production: Manganese	Ore(tons)	Metal(tons)	Value(£)
1880	40.00		80.00

            Comment 1880 STANNACOMBE
Ownership: 1879-1881 RICHARDS & POWER
Management: Chief Agent 1879-1881 W.H.HOSKING

Employment:		Underground	Surface	Total
	1879		1	1

103

	Underground	Surface	Total
1880	10		10

✳ STEEPERTON TOR   BELSTONE   SX 615884 0311

Production: Tin

	Black(tons)	Stuff(tons)	Tin(tons)	Value(£)
1878	1.00			34.40

Comment 1878 STEEPERTON

Ownership: 1877-1879 STEEPERTON MINING CO.LTD.; 1880-1882 STEEPERTON TOR MINING CO.LTD.
Comment 1880-1881 NOT WORKED

Management: Chief Agent 1875-1876 R.M.JEFFERY; 1877-1882 SML.ALDRIDGE Secretary 1875-1878 CHAS.LANGLEY&OTHERS; 1879 A.MOSES(LIQUIDATOR); 1880-1881 THOS.FICHUS

Employment:

	Underground	Surface	Total
1878	13	14	27
1879		1	1

STOCKLAND   BRAMSTON   0312

Production: Iron No detailed return
Management: Secretary 1875-1877 EDG.ALDOUS

STOKE GABRIEL   STOKE GABRIEL   0313

Production: Iron

	Ore(tons)	Iron(%)	Value(£)
1865	4000.00		1800.00
1866	790.00		256.70

Comment 1865-1866 BH.

STORMSDOWN   ASHBURTON   SX 768731 0314

Production: Copper

	Ore(tons)	Metal(tons)	Value(£)
1909	11.00		244.00

Comment 1909 INC.OWLACOMBE

Tin

	Black(tons)	Stuff(tons)	Tin(tons)	Value(£)
1895	2.00	60.00		60.00
1896	No detailed return			
1900	0.90			60.00
1905	2.30			209.00
1907	31.00			2910.00
1908	75.00			6120.00
1909	42.00			3252.00
1912	1.90			206.00
1913	5.20			800.00

Comment 1895 BLACK TIN ESTIMATED; 1900 LOCATION GIVEN AS BRIXHAM; 1907-1909 INC.OWLACOMBE; 1912-1913 INC.OWLACOMBE

Arsenic

	Ore(tons)	Metal(tons)	Value(£)
1896	2.00		45.00

Arsenic	Ore(tons)	Metal(tons)	Value(£)
1900	1.00		15.00
1905	5.00		29.00
1907	88.00		2243.00
1908	362.00		4337.00
1909	230.00		2760.00
1910	9.00		104.00
1913	55.00		400.00

Comment 1913 INC.OWLACOMBE

Ownership: 1895-1898 STORMSDOWN MINING CO.LTD.; 1899-1911 E.H.BAYLDON; 1912-1913 SIGFORD MINES LTD.
Comment 1898 IN LIQUIDATION; 1902 SUSPENDED; 1907-1910 INC.OWLACOMBE; 1911 INC.OWLACOMBE.DEVELOPMENT ONLY IN 1911; 1912 INC.OWLACOMBE.REOPENING JULY 1912; 1913 INC.OWLACOMBE.SUSPENDED APRIL 1913

Management: Chief Agent 1895-1898 H.A.MORRIS; 1906-1908 D.H.BAYLDON; 1909-1913 ERN.TERRELL
Secretary 1905-1909 D.H.BAYLDON; 1910-1911 G.A.HIGLETT

Employment:

	Underground	Surface	Total
1895	8		8
1896	9	10	19
1900		3	3
1901	4		4
1903	12	8	20
1904	14	16	30
1905	16	14	30
1906	22	70	92
1907	52	69	121
1908	54	67	121
1909	63	62	125
1910	6	4	10
1911	9	6	15
1912	11	9	20
1913	6	10	16

Comment 1907-1913 INC.OWLACOMBE

STOWFORD   NORTH MOLTON   SS 713319 0315

Production: Iron

	Ore(tons)	Iron(%)	Value(£)
1883	1545.00		425.00
1884	57.00		16.00
1885	No detailed return		
1886	10.00		5.00
1887	770.00		
1888	No detailed return		

Comment 1883-1888 RH.

Ownership: 1883-1884 NORTH MOLTON MINING CO.; 1885-1887 NORTH DEVON MINING CO.LTD.
Comment 1884 NOT WORKED IN 1884; 1887 INC.BAMPFYLDE

Management: Chief Agent 1883-1887 G.KEY KLINGENDER

Employment:

	Underground	Surface	Total
1883	6	3	9

STOWFORD   NORTH MOLTON   Continued

	Underground	Surface	Total
1885	3	2	5
1886	5		5
1887	8		8

Comment 1887 INC.BAMPFYLDE

SWINCOMBE VALE   LYDFORD   SX 647728 0316

Production: Tin No detailed return
Ownership: Comment 1873 STOPPED 1873
Management: Manager 1864-1867 W.V.WILLIAMS
            Chief Agent 1868-1873 JAS.WILLCOCKS
            Secretary 1868-1873 WM.VEAL

SYDENHAM   MARYSTOW   SX 438837 0317

Production: Manganese   Ore(tons) Metal(tons)   Value(£)

Year	Ore(tons)	Metal(tons)	Value(£)
1858-1860 No detailed return			
1870	23.40		102.70
1871	94.20		273.00

            Comment 1858-1860 SEE CHILLATON; 1870-1871 OR LEE WOOD
Ownership: 1909-1911 JAS.A.JOBLING
            Comment 1910-1911 SUSPENDED
Management: Chief Agent 1909-1911 WM.ARMSTRONG JNR.

TAMAR   BERE FERRERS   SX 424656 0318

Production: Lead & Silver   Ore(tons) Lead(tons) Silver(ozs)   Value(£)

Year	Ore(tons)	Lead(tons)	Silver(ozs)	Value(£)
1845	1454.00	944.00		
1846	1182.00	768.00		
1847	1082.00	649.00		
1848	1022.00	631.00		
1849	1106.00	636.00		
1850	977.00	561.80		
1851	1017.90	585.20		
1852	919.00	442.00	40200.00	
1853	840.00	429.00	36890.00	
1854	882.00	453.00	35330.00	
1860	781.50	585.00	8775.00	
1861	475.00	285.00	15902.00	
1863	210.10	133.00	6916.00	
1880	16.20	12.20	126.00	227.20

            Comment 1860-1861 TAMAR MINES

TAMAR CONSOLS   BERE FERRERS   SX 424656 0319

Production: Lead & Silver   Ore(tons) Lead(tons) Silver(ozs)   Value(£)

Year	Ore(tons)	Lead(tons)	Silver(ozs)	Value(£)
1855	728.00	372.00	305.00	

Management: Manager 1859-1861 JAS.WOLFERSTAN

          Chief Agent 1859 JOS.RICHARDS & THOS.FOOT; 1860-1861
          THOS.FOOT
          Secretary 1859-1861 JAS.WOLFERSTAN (P)

TAMAR CONSOLS   LIFTON   9999

Production: Lead & Silver   Ore(tons)   Lead(tons) Silver(ozs)   Value(£)
            1873   10.90   7.50   30.00   134.50
            Manganese No detailed return
Management: Chief Agent 1872-1873 GEO.ROWE; 1874-1879 WM.NEWTON &
            WM.DOIDGE
            Secretary 1872-1873 WM.NEWTON

TAMAR CONSOLS,EAST   BERE FERRERS   SX 437658 0320

Production: Lead & Silver   Ore(tons)   Lead(tons) Silver(ozs)   Value(£)
            1846   114.00   74.00
            1847   130.00   78.00
            1848   237.00   173.00
            1849   336.00   200.00
            1850   398.00   236.90
            1851   384.00   286.10
            1852   305.90   235.50   5226.00
            1853   228.00   166.00   3964.00
            1854   65.30   50.30   1075.00
            1855   25.00   17.00   408.00
            1856   4.50   3.50   123.00
            1857   20.00   13.50   756.00
            1858   113.00   71.80   3043.00
            1859   147.60   93.80   3484.00
            1860   53.00   33.70   1080.00
            1861   20.00   12.00   376.00
            Comment 1856 EAST TAMAR
Ownership: Comment 1862-1865 SUSPENDED
Management: Manager 1859 G.TREMAYNE
            Chief Agent 1859 G.TREMAYNE
            Secretary 1859 JAS.WOLFERSTAN (P); 1860-1861 T.V.LAWS (P);
            1862-1865 T.B.LAWS (P)

TAMAR CONSOLS,SOUTH   BERE ALSTON   SX 437645 0321

Production: Lead & Silver   Ore(tons)   Lead(tons) Silver(ozs)   Value(£)
            1849   176.00   123.00
            1850   477.00   340.00
            1851   668.00   474.00
            1852   950.40   684.80   41328.00
            1853   1068.00   654.00   56056.00
            1854   1469.90   964.70   61950.00
            1855   1325.40   716.00   59428.00
            1856   691.20   428.80   33351.00

Lead & Silver	Ore(tons)	Lead(tons)	Silver(ozs)	Value(£)
1857	83.00	36.50	2244.00	
1858	90.00	47.80	3200.00	
1859	58.00	31.00	2074.00	
1860	60.40	42.30	2834.00	
1861	No detailed return			

Comment 1856 MINE FLOODED ON 31ST.AUG. 1856

Ownership: Comment 1863-1865 SUSPENDED

Management: Manager 1860-1862 JAS.WOLFERSTAN
Chief Agent 1860 THOS.FOOT & J.TREVILLION; 1861-1862
THOS.FOOT
Secretary 1860-1861 JAS.WOLFERSTAN (P); 1862-1865 T.B.LAWS

✳ TAMAR SILVER LEAD   BERE FERRERS   SX 424656 0322➤

Production:

Lead & Silver	Ore(tons)	Lead(tons)	Silver(ozs)	Value(£)
1856	515.80	305.90	23104.00	
1857	591.00	332.50	22586.00	
1858	616.30	384.80	25476.00	
1859	842.80	580.00	40959.00	
1860	660.00	415.20	29103.00	
1861	524.50	363.80	19446.00	
1862	583.00	364.00	21690.00	
1881	10.00	7.70	60.00	125.00
1882	12.60	9.40	65.00	150.00

Fluorspar	Ore(tons)	Value(£)
1879	240.00	
1880	168.00	226.00
1881	250.00	175.00
1882	124.00	74.00

Comment 1879 TAMAR SILVER MINE

Ownership: 1878 RICH.GOLDSWORTHY; 1879 ENDEAN & CO.; 1880-1881 THE TAMAR
SILVER LEAD & FLUORSPAR CO.
Comment 1863-1865 SUSPENDED; 1880-1881 TAMAR SILVER LEAD &
FLUORSPAR

Management: Manager 1862 JAS.WOLFERSTAN
Chief Agent 1862 THOS.FOOT; 1879-1881 W.GOLDSWORTHY
Secretary 1862-1865 DUNSFORD&RANKIN (P); 1878 W.GOLDSWORTHY;
1880-1881 RICH.GOLDSWORTHY

✳ TAMAR VALLEY   BERE ALSTON   SX 437679 0323✳

Production:

Lead & Silver	Ore(tons)	Lead(tons)	Silver(ozs)	Value(£)
1870	39.60	29.70	116.00	
1871	No detailed return			
1872	16.40	12.00	48.00	
1873	12.30	8.40	360.00	146.00
1874	2.50	1.80	8.00	50.00
1875	19.60	14.40	115.00	347.30
1876	2.80	2.00		51.90

TAMAR VALLEY   BERE ALSTON   Continued

Fluorspar	Ore(tons)	Value(£)
1874	609.00	300.00
1875	280.00	140.00
1876	337.50	230.00
1885	49.00	49.00
1886	40.00	40.00

Comment 1874 TAMAR VALLEY SILVER LEAD; 1885-1886 NEW TAMAR VALLEY

Ownership: 1876 REPS.OF THE LATE GEO.PELL; 1878-1888 TAMAR VALLEY SILVER
              LEAD&FLOURSPAR CO.
              Comment 1886-1888 NEW TAMAR VALLEY
Management: Manager 1873-1875 S.TRURAN; 1876 HY.REYNOLDS
              Chief Agent 1868-1872 JOHN GOLDSWORTHY; 1878-1888
              RICH.GOLDSWORTHY
              Secretary 1868-1875 MAT.GREENE
Employment:

	Underground	Surface	Total
1878	10	2	12
1879	22	7	29
1880	17	11	28
1881	23	8	31
1882	14	6	20
1883	23	6	29
1886	10	2	12

 TAMAR,NORTH   BERE ALSTON   0324

Production: Lead & Silver No detailed return
Management: Manager 1873-1874 JNO.GOLDSWORTHY
              Chief Agent 1871-1872 JNO.GOLDSWORTHY; 1875-1876
              JNO.GOLDSWORTHY
              Secretary 1874 JAS.J.COWELL; 1875-1876 JAS.MYERSCOUGH & CO.

 TAVISTOCK GT. CONSOLS,E.   TAVISTOCK   0325

Production: Copper No detailed return
              Tin No detailed return
Ownership: 1881 TAVISTOCK CONSOLS MINING CO.
Management: Manager 1881 HY.TREGANOWAN
Employment:

	Underground	Surface	Total
1881	4		4

 TAVY CONSOLS   BUCKLAND MONACHORUM   SX 469688 0326

Production: Copper	Ore(tons)	Metal(tons)	Value(£)
1852	335.00	19.50	1635.60
1853	648.00	37.50	3516.20
1854	396.00	23.10	2234.20
1855	265.00	14.90	1383.30
1856	193.00	8.80	734.50
1857	530.00	23.60	2164.30

Copper	Ore(tons)	Metal(tons)	Value(£)
1858	268.00	11.70	991.80
1859	191.00	8.00	665.90
1860	156.00	8.40	734.80
1862	32.00	1.40	98.90
1863	17.00	0.60	35.70
1877	5.00	0.30	20.10
1879	23.60	1.30	62.00

Comment 1852-1860 (C); 1862-1863 (C)

Tin	Black(tons)	Stuff(tons)	Tin(tons)	Value(£)
1858	0.20			14.60

Arsenic Pyrite	Ore(tons)	Value(£)
1876	604.00	573.80
1877	41.40	26.00
1888	108.00	81.00
1890	1505.00	1125.00
1891	1300.00	250.00

Comment 1876 ARSENICAL MUNDIC; 1888 TAVY; 1890 TAVY; 1891
TAVY UNITED

Ownership: 1877-1880 JOS.BULKLEY; 1881-1883 JNO.PEARCE & HY.PEARCE;
1887-1890 TAVY MINING SYNDICATE; 1891-1892 TAVY UNITED MINES
& ARSENIC WORKS LTD.
Comment 1862-1865 SUSPENDED; 1882 NOT WORKED; 1883 NOT WORKED
IN 1883; 1887-1889 TAVY; 1890-1892 TAVY UNITED MINES &
ARSENIC WORKS

Management: Manager 1859 R.GOSS; 1860-1861 JOS.RICHARDS
Chief Agent 1859-1861 R.GOSS; 1875-1877 W.R.FOOTNER;
1879-1881 JOS.BULKLEY; 1887-1889 JOEL MANLEY; 1891-1892
CHAS.MASON
Secretary 1859-1865 THOS.FULLER (P); 1875-1876 JOS.BULKLEY;
1891-1892 ALF.E.CHAMPNERS (S)

Employment:

	Underground	Surface	Total
1879		2	2
1880-1881		1	1
1888	6		6
1889	6	3	9
1890	29	8	37
1891	12	34	46

TEIGN VALLEY   BRIDFORD   SX 830865 0327

Production: Lead No detailed return

Barytes	Ore(tons)	Value(£)
1855	35.00	
1877	976.00	3998.00
1878	312.70	1248.50
1880	30.00	15.00
1881	505.00	252.50
1882	500.00	263.00
1883	656.00	328.00
1884	593.00	300.00
1885	No detailed return	

Barytes	Ore(tons)	Value(£)
1886	800.00	400.00
1887	1000.00	500.00
1889	1200.00	700.00
1890	2000.00	1200.00
1891	2600.00	1560.00
1892	No detailed return	
1893	No detailed return	
1894	900.00	500.00
1895	500.00	250.00
1896	750.00	375.00

Comment 1855 BRIDFORD CONSOLS; 1878-1880 VALUE EST.;
1892-1893 INCLUDED IN DERBY TOTAL

Ownership: 1876-1880 TEIGN VALLEY LEAD&BARYTES CO.LTD.; 1881-1886 DEVON
BARYTES & CHEMICAL CO.; 1887-1888 BART.C.GIDLEY; 1889-1896
TEIGN VALLEY MINING CO.
Comment 1873 STOPPED 1873; 1888 SUSPENDED

Management: Manager 1870-1872 JOHN CORNISH; 1877 RICH.SOUTHEY
Chief Agent 1876 J.O.HARRIS; 1877-1880 JAS.ROWE; 1887-1888
BART.C.GIDLEY; 1889 JOSH.M.DURNSFORD; 1890-1896 M.DURNSFORD
Secretary 1870-1871 J.C.HARRIS; 1873-1875 J.O.HARRIS;
1877-1884 J.O.HARRIS (S); 1891-1896 M.J.DUNSFORD (S)

Employment:

	Underground	Surface	Total
1878	2	6	8
1881	2	2	4
1883	2	4	6
1884	4	4	8
1886	2	8	10
1887-1888	6	8	14
1889-1890	5	8	13
1891	5	11	16
1892	4	8	12
1893	3	7	10
1894	3	4	7
1895	2	2	4
1896		3	3

TEIGN VALLEY   GREAT WEEKE   SX 713875 0328

Production: Tin No detailed return
Ownership: 1896-1899 WM.ELLIS
Management: Chief Agent 1897-1899 SML.LEACH
Employment:

	Underground	Surface	Total
1896	6	4	10
1897	4	2	6
1898	13	5	18

THOMAS UNITED   CARDIGANSHIRE   0329

Production: Lead & Silver	Ore(tons)	Lead(tons)	Silver(ozs)	Value(£)
1854	70.00	54.00	1810.00	

TORBAY IRON   BRIXHAM

Production: Iron	Ore(tons)	Iron(%)	Value(£)
1870	1000.00		300.00
1871	3000.00		1700.00
1872	13000.00		7800.00
1874	No detailed return		
1875	300.00		225.00

Comment 1870 BH.; 1871 BH.TORBAY INC. SHARKHAM; 1872
BH.&CHINTER 5 ACRES & SHARKHAM; 1874 BH.SEE UPTON; 1875 BH.
Ownership: 1863-1866 TORBAY HAEMATITE IRON CO.; 1869 TORBAY IRON CO.;
1870-1871 RICHARDSON & CO.; 1872-1874 ODLING,EDWARDS &
TRIMNELL; 1875 C.READE & CO.
Comment 1872-1874 INC.CHINTER,FIVE ACRES & SHARKHAM
Management: Manager 1870-1874 RICH.CORNWALL
Chief Agent 1863 SML.RICHARDS; 1864-1866 ? PAULL; 1867-1869 ?
WINTLE; 1875 C.READE

TOY TOR   HELSTON, CORNWALL

Production: Tin No detailed return
Management: Manager 1869-1870 HY.MARTIN
Secretary 1869-1870 F.R.REEVES

TREEBY   PLYMPTON

Production: Tin No detailed return

TRUE BLUE   MINERA,DENBIGHSHIRE

Production: Lead & Silver	Ore(tons)	Lead(tons)	Silver(ozs)	Value(£)
1852	31.00	27.00	100.00	

UGBOROUGH   UGBOROUGH

Production: Iron	Ore(tons)	Iron(%)	Value(£)
1874	900.00		565.00
1875	1033.00		804.00
1876	300.00		225.50

Comment 1874-1876 BH.
Ownership: 1874-1876 HARRISON & SON
Management: Chief Agent 1875-1876 H.FORTESCUE HARRISON

UNITED DART MINES   BUCKFASTLEIGH

Production: Copper No detailed return
Ownership: Comment 1864-1865 SUSPENDED
Management: Chief Agent 1860-1863 HY.RICKARD
Secretary 1860-1865 E.SAWDYE (P)

Production: Copper No detailed return

Tin	Black(tons)	Stuff(tons)	Tin(tons)	Value(£)
1852	6.70			
1853	2.20			136.40
1854	23.50			1541.50
1855	28.70			1605.90
1856	12.80			844.70
1857	17.70			1289.60
1858	32.60			2002.20
1859	11.30			771.70
1860	25.60			1988.60
1861	11.50			832.90

Comment 1852 TAVISTOCK UNITED TIN ORE; 1853-1855 TAVISTOCK
UNITED; 1859-1861 UNITED TAVISTOCK
Ownership: Comment 1863-1865 SUSPENDED
Management: Chief Agent 1859-1860 JOHN TUCKER; 1861-1862 S.TUCKER
Secretary 1859 GEO.RICE (P); 1860-1862 ED.KING (P)

UPTON   BRIXHAM   0338

Iron	Ore(tons)	Iron(%)	Value(£)
1874	3419.00		2564.00
1875	2553.00		1914.00

Comment 1874 HE.INC.TORBAY IRON; 1875 HE.
Ownership: 1874 FRAN.EDWARDS & CO.; 1875-1876 UPTON HAEMATITE IRON ORE
CO.
Management: Manager 1875-1876 JAS.COCK
Chief Agent 1874 JNO.BROKENSHIRE

VICTORIA   ASHBURTON   SX 744716 0339

Production: Copper No detailed return
Ownership: Comment 1868-1870 SEE DRUID

VICTORIA,NEW   ASHBURTON   SX 744716 0340

Management: Manager 1869-1870 WM.SKEWIS
Chief Agent 1869-1870 MOSES BAWDEN
Secretary 1869-1870 JOHN G.BARRY

VIRTUOUS LADY   BUCKLAND MONACHORUM   SX 474698 0341

Copper	Ore(tons)	Metal(tons)	Value(£)
1870	112.00	6.10	301.70
1871	244.00	23.10	1455.20
1872	28.00	1.00	72.90

Comment 1870-1872 (C)

Tin	Black(tons)	Stuff(tons)	Tin(tons)	Value(£)
1871	2.00			156.50

Tin	Black(tons)	Stuff(tons)	Tin(tons)	Value(£)
1872	4.30			361.80

Ownership: Comment 1862-1865 SUSPENDED
Management: Manager 1859-1860 WM.GOSS; 1861 J.GOSS; 1868 HY.HORSWILL;
1869 H.HORSWILL & J.GIFFORD; 1870-1871 HY.HORSWILL; 1872
E.W.SECCOMBE; 1873 C.W.SECCOMBE; 1874-1876 E.W.SECCOMBE
Chief Agent 1869 JOHN TREWEEKE & W.WILLIAMS; 1870 J.TREWEEKE
& J.ROWE SNR.; 1871 J.TREWEEKE,J.ROWE SNR. & W.WILLIAMS
Secretary 1859-1860 JOS.RICHARDS (P); 1861-1865 E.COOK; 1868
H.DAINTY; 1869-1871 T.BARNARD; 1875-1876 HY.HORSWILL

✳ VITIFER CONSOLS,NEW   CHAGFORD   SX 678827 0342 ✳

Production: Copper No detailed return
Ownership: Comment 1873 VITIFER CONSOLS
Management: Manager 1869-1872 WM.RICHARDS; 1874-1875 JAS.BROWNING
Secretary 1873-1875 ED.G.CLARKE

VITIFER,EAST   NORTH BOVEY   SX 708823 0343

Production: Tin	Black(tons)	Stuff(tons)	Tin(tons)	Value(£)
1874	4.00			236.70
1875	12.80			632.40
1876	13.50			607.80
1877	1.30			50.00
1878	1.90			55.90
1879	1.00			34.30
1880	3.90			174.80
1881	1.10		0.80	62.00
1885	1.20			55.00
1886	0.70			36.00
1887	3.00			180.00
1888	No detailed return			

Ownership: 1877-1887 EAST VITIFER TIN MINING CO.LTD.; 1912-1913 EAST
VITIFER TIN CO. PER J.A.WYLIE
Comment 1883 NOT WORKED IN 1883; 1884 NOT WORKED IN 1884;
1913 SUSPENDED
Management: Manager 1872 R.MOORE; 1873-1874 HY.MINERS
Chief Agent 1872 R.JEFFRY; 1875-1878 JAS.BROWNING; 1879-1881
CHAS.H.MAUNDER; 1885-1886 CHAS.H.MAUNDER
Secretary 1872-1884 W.D.MANN; 1887 W.D.MANN

Employment:	Underground	Surface	Total
1878	4	1	5
1879	4	3	7
1880	15	7	22
1881	25	2	27
1885	8	1	9
1886	3	2	5
1887	4		4
1912-1913		6	6

WALKHAM AND POLDICE   TAVISTOCK   SX 493707 0344

Production: Lead   Ore(tons) Metal(tons)   Value(£)
            1865   4.90   3.20
            1866   No detailed return
            Copper   Ore(tons) Metal(tons)   Value(£)
            1866   25.00   1.10   90.00
            Comment 1866 (C)
            Tin   Black(tons) Stuff(tons)   Tin(tons)   Value(£)
            1865   1.10   61.50

WALKHAM UNITED   TAVISTOCK   SX 490708 0345

Production: Tin   Black(tons) Stuff(tons)   Tin(tons)   Value(£)
            1881   1.50   1.00   82.50
Ownership: 1881 WALKHAM UNITED MINES CO.LTD.
Management: Secretary 1881 J.W.GREENFIELD (P)
Employment: Underground   Surface   Total
            1881   16   9   25

WARD,SOUTH   BERE ALSTON   SX 427677 0346

Production: Lead & Silver   Ore(tons) Lead(tons) Silver(ozs)   Value(£)
            1873   56.70   39.20   156.00   1166.90
            1874   43.90   24.50   1386.00   597.60
            1875   21.80   8.10   547.00   236.50
            1876   1.50   1.10
Management: Manager 1868-1871 THOS.FOOT; 1875 RICH.GOLDSWORTHY
            Chief Agent 1872-1874 RICH.GOLDSWORTHY; 1876
            RICH.GOLDSWORTHY
            Secretary 1868-1876 THOS.HORSWILL

WATERMOUTH,GREAT   BERRYNARBOR   SS 573471 0347

Production: Lead & Silver No detailed return
Management: Chief Agent 1860-1868 JOHN TREWEEKE

WHIDDON   ASHBURTON   SX 757721 0348

Production: Tin No detailed return
Ownership: 1882 WHIDDON MINING CO.; 1885 WHIDDON MINING CO.
Management: Chief Agent 1882 JAS.BROWNING; 1885 PETER TERNBY
Employment: Underground   Surface   Total
            1882   2   2

WHIDDON   OKEHAMPTON   0349

Production: Copper No detailed return
            Tin No detailed return
            Wolfram No detailed return

Ownership: 1911-1913 J.P.BARKER
             Comment 1911 PROSPECTING FROM DEC.1911; 1912 SUSPENDED
             DEC.1911; 1913 SUSPENDED WIDDON
Employment: Underground   Surface   Total
             1911   3   3

WHITEWORKS   PRINCETOWN   SX 612708 0350

Production: Tin   Black(tons) Stuff(tons) Tin(tons)   Value(£)
             1871   9.10   703.30
             1872   18.00   1602.10
             1874   18.00   820.00
             1875   24.70   1424.10
             1876   16.10   691.50
            Comment 1874 VALUE EST.
Ownership: Comment 1875-1876 NEW WHITEWORKS
Management: Manager 1869-1871 WM.SKEWIS; 1874 WM.SKEWIS
            Chief Agent 1869-1871 JOHN ROSEWARNE; 1875-1876 JOHN
            ROSEWARNE
            Secretary 1869-1871 HY.BARTON; 1872 J.BARRY; 1874-1876
            T.H.HITCHENS

WHITLEIGH   TAMERTON FOLIOTT   SX 483598 0351

Production: Lead & Silver   Ore(tons) Lead(tons) Silver(ozs)   Value(£)
             1854   No detailed return
             1855   54.00   30.00   1410.00
             1856   7.80   5.20
             1857   No detailed return
            Comment 1854 SEE WHITLEIGH, CORNWALL; 1856 FOR AG SEE
            CARPENTER

WHITSTONE   BRENTOR   SX 464818 0352

Production: Manganese   Ore(tons) Metal(tons)   Value(£)
             1881   41.00   50.00
             1883   20.00   50.00
             1884-1886 No detailed return
            Ochre No detailed return
Ownership: 1880-1881 MANGANESE MINING CO.; 1884-1886 W.PETHYBRIDGE &
            CO.; 1887-1904 WHITSTONE MINE CO.
            Comment 1890-1893 SUSPENDED; 1894-1902 ONLY OCCASIONAL WORK
            DONE
Management: Chief Agent 1880-1881 W.PETHYBRIDGE; 1887-1888 W.PETHYBRIDGE
            & CO.; 1889-1904 THOS.C.REED
            Secretary 1884-1886 T.C.REED; 1889-1890 W.PETHYBRIDGE & CO.
Employment: Underground   Surface   Total
             1880   4   4
             1881   2   2
             1884   2   2

	Underground	Surface	Total
1885	6	6	12
1886-1887		1	1
1888		2	2
1889-1891		1	1
1894		2	2
1895	1	1	2
1896-1897		1	1
1898		2	2
1900	1		1
1901-1902		2	2
1903-1904		1	1

WOLBOROUGH   NEWTON ABBOT   SX 839698 0353

Production: Iron	Ore(tons)	Iron(%)	Value(£)
1870	240.20		124.00
1874	1000.00		750.00

Comment 1870 BH.; 1874 BH.WALBOROUGH
Ownership: 1874-1876 LOWTHER IRON ORE CO.
Management: Chief Agent 1874-1876 W.H.HOSKING

WOLSTON'S IRON PAINT   BRIXHAM   0354

Production: Iron	Ore(tons)	Iron(%)	Value(£)
1860	80.00		32.00
1861	74.00		29.60

Comment 1860-1861 BH.
Ownership: 1863-1865 R.W.WOLSTON
Management: Chief Agent 1864-1865 CAPT.DENNIS

WOOD MINE   SX 476661 0355

Production: Lead	Ore(tons)	Metal(tons)	Value(£)
1852	3.50	2.60	
1856	4.70	3.00	
1857	4.50	3.00	

Comment 1856 FOR AG SEE CARPENTER

WREY CONSOLS   BUCKFASTLEIGH   SX 716684 0356

Production: Tin No detailed return
Ownership: Comment 1864-1865 SUSPENDED
Management: Chief Agent 1860-1863 W.O.WILLIAMS

Production: Iron No detailed return
Ownership: 1875-1877 PADDESON & CO.
Management: Chief Agent 1875-1877 WM.RICHARDS

YARNER BOVEY TRACEY SX 783783 0358

Production: Copper	Ore(tons)	Metal(tons)	Value(£)
1858	155.00	5.00	400.00
1861	411.00	15.20	1240.70
1862	594.00	23.40	1820.70
1863	414.00	15.70	1084.90
1864	379.00	13.30	1122.30
1865	118.00	3.70	295.00

Comment 1858 (C); 1861-1865 (C)
Ownership: Comment 1865 SUSPENDED; 1866-1867 SEE DEVON FRANCES; 1868 OR DEVON FRANCES
Management: Manager 1859-1860 JAS.HAMPTON; 1861-1864 R.BARKELL
Chief Agent 1859-1860 JOHN MIDDLETON; 1861 JAS.HAMPTON; 1868 W.WILLIAMS
Secretary 1859-1863 C.WESTCOMBE (P); 1864 W.G.NORRIS

YEALMPTON YEALMPTON 0359

Production: Iron	Ore(tons)	Iron(%)	Value(£)
1867	250.00		81.20

Comment 1867 BH.
Ownership: 1872 WM.BROWNE

YEO MILLS CHAGFORD 0360

Ownership: 1893 JAS.NEILL & CO.
Comment 1893 EXPLORATION
Management: Chief Agent 1893 JAS.NEILL

YEOLAND CONSOLS HORRABRIDGE SX 514663 0361

Production: Tin	Black(tons)	Stuff(tons)	Tin(tons)	Value(£)
1852	44.70			
1853	72.20			4717.40
1854	75.00			4500.00
1855	46.80			2411.70
1856	34.30			2552.20
1857	19.00			1550.10
1883	7.50			412.00
1884	7.70			325.00
1885	29.50			1462.00
1886	54.80			3060.00
1887	46.50			2797.00
1888	31.60			2139.00

Comment 1852 TIN ORE
Ownership: 1881-1892 YEOLAND CONSOLS MINING CO.LTD.
            Comment 1887 IN LIQUIDATION; 1890-1891 SUSPENDED; 1892
            ABANDONED OWNERS GONE TO AMERICA
Management: Chief Agent 1881-1884 JOEL MANLEY; 1885-1886 JOHN BEARE;
            1891-1892 E.A.RICH
            Secretary 1887-1890 E.A.RICH
Employment:

	Underground	Surface	Total
1881	6	2	8
1882	6	8	14
1883	15	15	30
1884	6	26	32
1885	25	25	50
1886	30	27	57
1887	29	22	51
1888	15	15	30
1889		1	1

YEOLAND,SOUTH   HORRABRIDGE   SX 513660 0362

Production: Tin   Black(tons) Stuff(tons)   Tin(tons)   Value(£)
            1854   4.30   230.60

YETLAND   COMBEMARTIN   SS 579450 0363

Production: Lead No detailed return
Ownership: Comment 1878-1879 CLOSED APRIL 1878
Management: Chief Agent 1876-1879 FRANK TOMS
            Secretary 1876-1879 FRANK TOMS

ZEAL CONSOLS,SOUTH   SOUTH TAWTON   0364

Production: Copper No detailed return
Management: Chief Agent 1860-1868 J.TREE
            Secretary 1860-1868 R.BROOK (P)

SUNDRIES   0365

Production: Lead   Ore(tons) Metal(tons)   Value(£)
            1847   50.00   25.00
            Zinc   Ore(tons) Metal(tons)   Value(£)
            1866   135.00   236.30
            1867   97.00   242.00
            1868   69.00   172.50
            1869   87.30   251.00
            Comment 1866-1869 SUNDRY SMALL LOTS; 1868-1869 TOTAL, SHIPPED
            AT TEIGNMOUTH
            Copper   Ore(tons) Metal(tons)   Value(£)
            1854   644.00   53.60   5657.90

119

Comment 1854 (S)

Manganese	Ore(tons)	Metal(tons)	Value(£)
1861	925.80		2925.50
1869	1558.20		7897.80

Comment 1861 TAVISTOCK & LAUNCESTON MINES; 1869 BETWEEN TAVISTOCK & LAUNCESTON

Iron	Ore(tons)	Iron(%)	Value(£)
1870	750.00		190.00
1871	800.00		600.00

Comment 1870-1871 BH.

Section B

The Somerset

Returns

```
Production: Lead No detailed return
Ownership:  1905 WITHERS & BROWN
            Comment 1905 SINKING
Employment:             Underground    Surface      Total
            1905            3                          3
```

ASHTON HILL   BRISTOL   0002

Production: Iron	Ore(tons)	Iron(%)	Value(£)
1858	2000.00		1000.00
1859	750.00		475.00
1860-1864 No detailed return			
1865	620.00		310.00
1866	635.00		317.50
1867-1868 No detailed return			
1869	626.00		219.10
1870	2110.00		738.20
1871	2654.60		2654.60
1872	2000.00		1500.00
1873	15800.00		11850.00

```
            Comment 1858-1860 HE.; 1861 HE.SEE ASHTON VALE; 1862 HE.;
            1863 HE.SEE SUNDRIES; 1864 HE.SEE ASHTON VALE; 1865-1873 HE.
Ownership:  1863-1869 ASHTON VALE IRON CO.; 1870-1873 ASHTON VALE IRON
            CO.LTD.
Management: Chief Agent 1863-1869 E.KNIGHT & CO.; 1870-1873 A.RICHARDS
```

ASHTON VALE   BRISTOL   0003

Production: Iron	Ore(tons)	Iron(%)	Value(£)
1858	2616.00		1308.00
1859	2000.00		950.00
1860	3960.00		1980.00
1861	7300.00		3650.00
1862	342.00		85.20
1863	No detailed return		
1864	12965.00		6482.50
1865	6348.00		3174.00
1866	2720.00		1360.00
1867	2350.00		940.00
1868	2760.00		
1869	1646.00		577.60
1870	2051.30		717.50
1871	1673.00		1673.00
1872	No detailed return		
1873	620.10		469.80
1874	952.50		714.50
1875	1015.00		431.20

```
            Comment 1858-1860 AC.; 1861 AC.INC.ASHTON HILL; 1862 AC.;
            1863 AC.SEE SUNDRIES; 1864 AC.INC.ASHTON HILL; 1865-1866 AC.;
            1867 AC.ASHTON VALE COLLIERY; 1868-1871 AC.; 1872 AC.SEE
            SUNDRIES; 1873-1875 AC.
```

ASHTON VALE   BRISTOL   Continued

Ownership: 1863-1869 ASHTON VALE IRON CO.; 1870-1878 ASHTON VALE IRON
             CO.LTD.
Management: Chief Agent 1863-1869 E.KNIGHT & CO.; 1870-1878 A.RICHARDS

BERTHA   NUNNEY AND WHACLEY   0004

Production: Manganese No detailed return
             Iron No detailed return
Ownership: 1904 WHEAL BERTHA IRON & MANGANESE PROP.CO.
Management: Chief Agent 1904 GEO.SPARGO

BLACKLAND   MINEHEAD   SS 841367 0005

Production: Iron   Ore(tons)   Iron(%)   Value(£)
            1875   134.00   100.00
             Comment 1875 AC.
Ownership: 1875-1881 EXFORD IRON ORE CO.
Management: Manager 1875 RICH.GARDNER CRIPPS; 1877-1878 WM.GIBBS
             Chief Agent 1876 RICH.GARDNER CRIPPS; 1879-1880 JOHN ARGALL
             JNR

BLACKMOOR   BLAGDON   0006

Production: Lead No detailed return
Ownership: 1883-1886 R.NICHOLS
             Comment 1867-1872 SEE CHARTERHOUSE; 1875-1882 SEE
             CHARTERHOUSE; 1883-1886 BLACKMORE

BRENDON HILLS   WATCHET   ST 025344 0007

Production:	Iron	Ore(tons)	Iron(%)	Value(£)
	1858	19018.00		9509.00
	1859	23183.40		11591.50
	1860	18072.70		9036.40
	1861	23787.80		11893.90
	1862	29321.10		14660.10
	1863	23582.00		11791.00
	1864	28825.80		14412.90
	1865	27541.60		13770.80
	1866	29468.10		14734.00
	1867	32524.90		16262.50
	1868	27925.00		
	1869	23458.00		6658.10
	1870	14603.00		5111.00
	1871	27556.00		27556.00
	1872	27913.40		27913.00
	1873	28982.00		28982.00
	1874	38316.50		28316.50
	1875	41792.80		31346.00

Iron	Ore(tons)	Iron(%)	Value(£)
1876	41351.00		28945.70
1877	46894.80		32825.80
1878	40115.30		28080.70
1879	14100.00		10147.50
1880	27668.00		22134.40
1881	26265.00		21012.00
1882	31354.00	34.60	23515.00
1883	10081.00		7561.00
1908	2550.00	55.00	1800.00

Comment 1858-1862 SP.BRENDON & EISEN HILL; 1863-1864 SP.;
1865-1871 SP.BRENDON & EISEN HILLS; 1872-1883 SP.; 1908 SP.
Ownership: 1863-1876 BRENDON HILLS IRON ORE CO.; 1877-1883 EBBW VALE
STEEL IRON&COAL CO.LTD.; 1907-1908 SOMERSET MINERAL SYNDICATE
LTD.; 1909-1910 WATCHET BRIQUETTING SYNDICATE LTD.
Comment 1875-1876 INC.EISEN HILL; 1909 COTTON MINE; 1910
COTTON MINE CLOSED DEC.1909
Management: Manager 1875-1881 HY.SKEWIS; 1907-1908 H.B.SMITH
Chief Agent 1863-1866 MGN.MORGAN; 1867-1874 HY.SKEWIS; 1883
HY.SKEWIS; 1909-1910 S.C.WRIGHT
Employment:

	Underground	Surface	Total
1883	50	37	87
1907	41	31	72
1908	72	45	117
1909	15	25	40

CARBON   WEST HARPTREE   0008

Production: Barytes No detailed return
Ochre No detailed return
Ownership: 1906-1907 KINGSWAY SYNDICATE LTD.
Comment 1907 SUSPENDED JAN.1908
Employment:

	Underground	Surface	Total
1906	8	7	15
1907	6	4	10

CHARTERHOUSE   BLAGDON   0009

Production: Lead No detailed return
Ownership: 1859 MENDIP MINING CO.; 1860-1883 MENDIP MINING CO.LTD.
Comment 1859-1866 REWORKED TIPS; 1867-1872 REWORKED TIPS
INC.UBLEY & BLACKMOOR; 1873-1874 REWORKED TIPS INC.UBLEY;
1875-1883 REWORKED TIPS INC.BLACKMOOR
Management: Manager 1865-1874 JOS.MURRAY; 1875-1881 WM.RODGER
Chief Agent 1859-1861 H.HORNBLOWER; 1862-1864 MR DERRICK;
1871-1874 WM.RODGER

CHEWTON MINERY

Ownership: 1859 E.H.BARWELL & CO.; 1860-1866 E.H.BARWELL & WRIGHT
              Comment 1859-1866 REWORKED TIPS
Management: Chief Agent 1859-1866 J.BRAY

COLTON   WASHFORD   ST 053352 0011

Production:	Iron	Ore(tons)	Iron(%)	Value(£)
	1909	920.00	44.20	690.00

DOLBERROW   LYNCOMBE   0012

Production:	Iron	Ore(tons)	Iron(%)	Value(£)
	1880	450.00		270.00

EISEN HILL   WATCHET   SS 905372 0013

Production:	Iron	Ore(tons)	Iron(%)	Value(£)
	1858-1862 No detailed return			
	1863	8627.00		4313.50
	1864	7560.00		4536.00
	1865-1871 No detailed return			

              Comment 1858-1862 SP.SEE BRENDON HILLS; 1863-1864 SP.;
              1865-1871 SP.SEE BRENDON HILLS
Ownership: 1863-1874 BRENDON HILLS IRON ORE CO.
              Comment 1875-1876 SEE BRENDON HILLS
Management: Chief Agent 1863-1866 MGN.MORGAN; 1867-1874 HY.SKEWIS

EXFORD   SEXFORD   0014

Production:	Iron	Ore(tons)	Iron(%)	Value(£)
	1874	10.00		7.50
	1877	1000.00		700.00

              Comment 1874 SP.3000 TONS RAISED; 1877 BH.IN STOCK
              Pyrites No detailed return
Ownership: 1874-1875 EXFORD IRON ORE CO.; 1878-1881 WM.GIBBS
Management: Manager 1874-1875 RICH.GARDNER CRIPPS
              Chief Agent 1880-1881 JOHN H.MILES

EXMOOR   EXMOOR   SS 797378 0015

Production:	Iron	Ore(tons)	Iron(%)	Value(£)
	1910	250.00	56.00	125.00
	1911	200.00	55.00	75.00
	1912	400.00	55.00	200.00
	1913	850.00	55.00	276.00

Ownership: 1909 SEE EXMOOR, DEVON; 1910-1913 EXMOOR MINING SYNDICATE
Management: Chief Agent 1910-1913 HY.ROBERTS

Employment:

	Underground	Surface	Total
1910	10	5	15
1911	9	9	18
1912	10	6	16
1913	12	8	20

FULLABROOK   BRAUNTON, DEVON   SS 515398 0016

Production: Manganese No detailed return
Ownership: 1877-1881 JOS.POPE
           Comment 1877-1881 DEVON MINE
Management: Chief Agent 1880-1881 JOS.POPE

FURZE HILL   HORRABRIDGE, DEVON   SX 516692 0017

Production: Tin No detailed return
Ownership: 1877-1879 WM.DOIDGE
           Comment 1877-1879 DEVON?
Management: Manager 1877-1879 WM.DOIDGE

HAM   SHEPTON MALLET   0018

Production: Iron No detailed return
Ownership: Comment 1864-1867 RETURNED WITH NO DETAILS

HARPTREE WORKS,EAST   RADSTOCK   0019

Production: Lead No detailed return
Ownership: 1867-1868 EAST HARPTREE LEAD MINING CO.; 1869-1870 WALDEGRAVE
           LEAD SMELTING CO.; 1877-1882 EAST HARPTREE LEAD CO.; 1883
           BOLTON & CO.
           Comment 1866-1874 REWORKED TIPS; 1875 REWORKED TIPS IN
           LIQUIDATION
Management: Manager 1867-1872 J.BRAY; 1874-1875 WM.PANNELL
           Chief Agent 1866 J.DANIEL; 1873 WM.PANNELL
           Secretary 1867-1870 THOS.KINSMAN (S); 1871-1875 WM.H.BUMPUS
           (S)

HARPTREE,EAST   RADSTOCK   0020

Production: Iron   Ore(tons)   Iron(%)   Value(£)
            1880   100.00   60.00
            Comment 1880 BH.HARPTREE EAST & WEST
Ownership: 1874 COUNTESS OF WALDEGRAVE; 1875-1876 EAST HARPTREE LEAD
           MINING CO.; 1877 J.NICHOLS; 1878-1879 HARPTREE CO.; 1880-1881
           BOLTON & BEWICK; 1883-1886 BOLTON & CO.
Management: Chief Agent 1878-1882 J.NICHOLS

Production: Manganese   Ore(tons) Metal(tons)   Value(£)
            1890   30.00   59.00
            1891   50.00   75.00
            Comment 1890-1891 HIGHER PITTS
            Iron   Ore(tons)   Iron(%)   Value(£)
            1891-1893 No detailed return
            Comment 1891-1893 ORE PRODUCER
Ownership: 1891-1893 SOMERSETSHIRE MANGANESE IRON CO.LTD.

HONEYMEAD   0022

Production: Iron   Ore(tons)   Iron(%)   Value(£)
            1858   500.00   250.00
            1859   No detailed return
            Comment 1858-1859 SP.

LODMORE POOL AND HAYDEN   MENDIPS   0023

Production: Iron No detailed return
Management: Chief Agent 1874-1875 EDM.LLOYD OWEN

LUCKYARD   EXFORD   0024

Production: Iron No detailed return
Ownership: 1876 EXFORD IRON ORE CO.
Management: Manager 1876 RICH.GARDNER CRIPPS

MALAGO VALE   WINFORD   0025

Production: Iron No detailed return
            Ochre No detailed return
            401234140012 No detailed return
Ownership: 1884-1886 BOLTON & CO.; 1887-1888 BOLTON & PARTNERS LTD.

MELLS   FROME   0026

Production: Iron No detailed return
Management: Chief Agent 1874 W.B.NAIST

MENDIP HILLS   WELLS   0027

Production: Iron   Ore(tons)   Iron(%)   Value(£)
            1873   118.30   88.00
            1874   57.30   45.00
            Comment 1873-1874 BH.
Ownership: 1873 WALDEGRAVE MINING CO.
Management: Manager 1873 THOS.KINSMAN

PARRACOMBE, DEVON   SPARRACOMBE   0028

Production: Lead & Silver No detailed return
Ownership: 1877 CHAS.MAUNDER & CO.
Management: Manager 1877 CHAS.MAUNDER

PRIDDEY   0029

Production: Lead No detailed return
Ownership: 1859 N.ENNOR & CO.; 1860-1865 WEST OF ENGLAND SMELTING
            CO.LTD.
            Comment 1859-1865 REWORKED TIPS
Management: Chief Agent 1859 N.ENNOR; 1860-1861 M.THOMAS; 1862-1865
            H.HORNBLOWER

RED HOUSE   WINFORD   0030

Production: Iron   Ore(tons)   Iron(%)   Value(£)
            1875   1240.00   930.00
            1881   2911.00   800.50
            Comment 1875 RH.; 1881 BH.
            Ochre No detailed return
            401234140012 No detailed return
Ownership: 1881 WINFORD IRON ORE & REDDING CO.LTD.; 1887-1913 WINFORD
            IRON ORE & REDDING CO.LTD.
Management: Chief Agent 1881 WM.ARGALL; 1913 S.TAYLOR
Employment: Underground   Surface   Total
            1894-1898   1   1
            1899   2   2
            1900   1   1
            1901-1904   2   2
            1905-1906   3   3
            1907   4   4
            1908-1909   3   2   5
            1910-1913   4   2   6

REGIL   WINFORD   0031

Production: Lead No detailed return
            Iron   Ore(tons)   Iron(%)   Value(£)
            1888   No detailed return
            1890-1892 No detailed return
            Comment 1888 SEE ECTON STAFFORDSHIRE; 1889 ORE PRODUCER
            Ochre No detailed return
            401234140012 No detailed return
Ownership: 1887-1895 REGIL MINING CO.; 1896-1900 HEMINGWAY & CO.;
            1901-1913 REGIL MINING CO.
            Comment 1913 SUSPENDED
Management: Chief Agent 1901-1913 WM.ARGALL
            Secretary 1901-1913 COLTHURST & HARDING
Employment: Underground   Surface   Total
            1894   10   8   18

                                      129

	Underground	Surface	Total
1895	7	8	15
1896	4	5	9
1897	6	7	13
1898	5	4	9
1899	7	5	12
1900	4	4	8
1901-1903	5		5
1904	4		4
1905	5		5
1906	4	4	8
1907	4		4
1908	2		2
1909-1910	1	1	2
1911-1913		1	1

RIDGE HILL NO.1   WINFORD   0032

Production: Iron	Ore(tons)	Iron(%)	Value(£)
1881	100.00		60.00
1882	300.00		225.00
1883	250.00		187.00
1884	104.00		11.00
1885	97.00		10.00
1886	45.00		
1887	558.00		

            Comment 1881-1887 BH.
Ownership: 1880-1886 MICH.HOBBS

RIDGE HILL NO.2   WINFORD   0033

Production: Lead No detailed return
            Iron No detailed return
Ownership: 1880-1886 CHAS.PIERCE
Management: Chief Agent 1880-1881 CHAS.PIERCE

RIDGE HILL NO.3   WINFORD   0034

Production: Iron No detailed return
Ownership: 1881-1882 ALF.KING
Management: Chief Agent 1881 ALF.KING

ROSE   EXBRIDGE   SS 934243 0035

Production: Manganese	Ore(tons)	Metal(tons)	Value(£)
1881	40.00		96.30
1882	95.00		65.00

            Comment 1881 MANGONIFEROUS IRON ORE
            Iron No detailed return

ROSE   EXBRIDGE   Continued

Ownership: 1881 JOHN GUNN
Management: Chief Agent 1881 W.W.BABB

ROWBOROUGH   BLAGDON   0036

Production: Iron No detailed return
            Ochre No detailed return
            401234140012 No detailed return
Ownership: 1880-1884 W.WOOKEY; 1886-1887 W.WOOKEY; 1889-1894 W.WOOKEY
            Comment 1887 DOWBOROUGH; 1889-1892 DOWBOROUGH; 1893-1894
            DOWBOROUGH SUSPENDED

SOMERSET MINES   RADSTOCK   0037

Production: Iron   Ore(tons)   Iron(%)   Value(£)
            1874   1506.00   1129.50
            Comment 1874 BH.
Ownership: 1874-1875 SOMERSET IRON ORE CO.; 1876-1880 SOMERSET IRON CO.;
            1881-1882 SOMERSET IRON ORE CO.
            Comment 1878 SOMERSET

ST. CUTHBERTS WORKS   PRIDDY   0038

Production: Lead   Ore(tons) Metal(tons)   Value(£)
            1890   182.00   140.00   1008.00
            1891   80.00   43.00   356.00
            1892   108.00   61.00   481.00
            1893   480.00   50.00   1440.00
            1894   691.00   364.00   2375.00
            Comment 1890 WRONGLY LISTED AS DEVON; 1892-1894 OPENWORK
Ownership: 1869-1875 ST.CUTHBERT LEAD SMELTING CO.; 1883 J.E.WATTS
            Comment 1869-1874 REWORKING TIPS; 1875 REWORKING TIPS IN
            LIQUIDATION; 1883 ST.CUTHBERTS LEAD WORKS
Management: Chief Agent 1869-1875 W.FORGAN

STALLARDS   WINFORD   0039

Production: Iron   Ore(tons)   Iron(%)   Value(£)
            1880   125.00   78.00
            1881   60.00   36.00
            Comment 1880 BH.TALLARDS; 1881 BH.
Ownership: 1880-1883 EDM.LLOYD OWEN
Management: Chief Agent 1880 EDM.LLOYD OWEN

TAR HALL   0040

Production: Lead No detailed return
Ownership: 1859 E.H.BARWELL & CO.; 1860-1865 E.H.BARWELL & WRIGHT

131

TAR HALL   Continued

        Comment 1859-1865 REWORKED TIPS
Management: Chief Agent 1859-1865 J.BRAY

TARN   WINFORD   0041

Production: Iron   Ore(tons)   Iron(%)   Value(£)
            1880   50.00   30.00
            Comment 1880 BH.

TEMPLE CLOUD   BRISTOL   0042

Production: Iron   Ore(tons)   Iron(%)   Value(£)
            1876   186.00   139.00
            1877   33.00   23.00
            Comment 1876 SP.; 1877 BH.
Ownership: 1880-1881 JOHN HIPPLESBY

THORNE,LOWER   EXFORD   0043

Production: Iron No detailed return
            Umber No detailed return
Ownership: 1878-1881 JOHN H.MILES
Management: Manager 1878 JOHN H.MILES

TREBOROUGH   TREBOROUGH   0044

Production: Iron No detailed return
Ownership: 1904 SIR W.T.TREVELYAN
Management: Chief Agent 1904 E.HELLARD

TWO WATERS MEET   WINFORD   0045

Production: Iron No detailed return
Ownership: 1875-1878 CAMERON & DUNCAN
Management: Chief Agent 1875-1878 JOHN COMER

UBLEY   WELLS   0046

Production: Lead No detailed return
Ownership: 1877-1883 CHARTERHOUSE MINING CO.
            Comment 1867-1874 SEE CHARTERHOUSE

WALDEGRAVE WORKS   CHEWTON MENDIP   0047

Production: Lead No detailed return
            Iron No detailed return

Ownership: 1867-1868 MENDIP MINING CO.LTD.; 1869-1877 WALDEGRAVE LEAD
             SMELTING CO.; 1878 MESSRS.BROOKE & CO.; 1879-1881 TRUSTEE OF
             COUNTESS OF WALDEGRAVE; 1883 BOLTON & PTNS
             Comment 1866 SEE CHEWTON MINERY; 1867-1881 REWORKING TIPS
Management: Manager 1867-1875 J.BRAY
             Chief Agent 1877-1878 THOS.KINSMAN; 1879-1881 J.MCMURTRIE
             Secretary 1869-1876 THOS.KINSMAN (S)

WINFORD NO.1   FLAX BOURTON   0048

Production: Iron   Ore(tons)   Iron(%)   Value(£)
            1883   4064.00   3048.00
            1884   3478.00   2608.00
            1885   2002.00   1500.00
            1886   3986.00
            1887   840.00
            Comment 1888-1893 ORE PRODUCER
Ownership: 1875-1876 WINFORD IRON ORE CO.; 1877-1883 WINFORD IRON ORE &
            REDDING CO.LTD.; 1886-1888 WINFORD IRON ORE & REDDING
            CO.LTD.; 1889-1893 WINFORD IRON ORE CO.LTD.
Management: Chief Agent 1875-1880 J.SHERBURN
            Secretary 1877-1878 J.T.GROOM (S); 1881 S.TAYLOR

WINFORD NO.2   WINFORD   0049

Production: Iron   Ore(tons)   Iron(%)   Value(£)
            1875   184.00   41.40
            1880   925.00   555.00
            1881   147.00   88.20
            Comment 1875 RH.MICHAEL HOBBS; 1880 BH.MICHAEL HOBBS; 1881
            BH.WINFORD MICHAEL HOBBS
Ownership: 1875-1877 MICH.HOBBS; 1881 MICH.HOBBS
            Comment 1875 RIDGE HILL NO 1?
Management: Chief Agent 1875-1877 MICH.HOBBS; 1881 MICH.HOBBS

WINFORD NO.3   WINFORD   0050

Production: Iron   Ore(tons)   Iron(%)   Value(£)
            1881   400.00   240.00
            Comment 1881 BH.WINFORD CHARLES PEARCE
Ownership: 1875 CHAS.PIERCE; 1881 CHAS.PIERCE
            Comment 1875 RIDGE HILL NO 2   .
Management: Chief Agent 1881 CHAS.PIERCE

WINFORD NO.4   WINFORD   0051

Production: Barytes   Ore(tons)   Value(£)
            1882   10.00   5.00
            1883   No detailed return

Manganese	Ore(tons)	Metal(tons)	Value(£)
1884	11.00		16.00
1885	No detailed return		
1895	2.00		1.00

Iron	Ore(tons)	Iron(%)	Value(£)
1887	86.00		
1888-1893	No detailed return		

Comment 1888-1893 ORE PRODUCER
Ochre No detailed return
401234140012 No detailed return
Ownership: 1880-1883 W.BROAD; 1884-1886 H.C.BURGE; 1887-1893 SLOWMAN
H.C.BURGE

WINFORD NO.5   WINFORD   0052

Production: Iron No detailed return
Ownership: 1880-1886 ALF.KING

WINFORD NO.6   BRISTOL   0053

Production: Iron No detailed return
Ownership: 1875 OWEN & FIRMSTONE
Management: Chief Agent 1875 H.OWEN

WINFORD NO.7   BRISTOL   0054

Production: Iron No detailed return
Ownership: 1875-1876 DAWBARN & CO.

WINFORD NO.8   BRISTOL   0055

Production: Iron No detailed return
Management: Chief Agent 1877 WM.ARGALL

YATTON   0056

Production: Iron	Ore(tons)	Iron(%)	Value(£)
1858	707.40		353.70
1859	1580.20		790.10
1860	569.10		284.50
1861	175.40		87.70
1862	74.30		37.20

Comment 1858 BH.SEVERAL MENDIP MINES; 1859 BH.; 1860
BH.BRISTOL & EXETER RLY.ONLY; 1861 BH.; 1862 BH.BRISTOL &
EXETER RLY.ONLY

Production: Iron	Ore(tons)	Iron(%)	Value(£)
1858	1200.00		600.00
1859	1570.00		695.00
1860	1500.00		750.00
1861	1500.00		750.00
1862	1750.00		437.50
1863	2500.00		1250.00
1864	3500.00		1400.00
1865	3475.00		1737.50
1866	2500.00		1250.00
1867	2000.00		750.00
1868	1765.00		
1869	1500.00		525.00
1870	975.00		341.20
1871	1000.00		1000.00
1872	1000.00		750.00
1873	1012.00		759.00
1874	500.00		375.00
1875	550.00		275.00

Comment 1858-1862 AC.; 1863 AC.INC.ASHTON HILL&ASHTON VALE;
1864-1865 AC.; 1866 AC.COLLIERIES NR.BRISTOL; 1867-1870
AC.BRISTOL COALFD.SUND.PARCELS; 1871 AC.; 1872 AC.INC.ASHTON
VALE; 1873-1875 AC.

Production: Iron	Ore(tons)	Iron(%)	Value(£)
1875	250.00		62.50
1876	2762.10		2025.40
1877	4000.00		2800.00
1878	3000.00		2100.00
1882	4413.00		3310.00
1888	1388.00	34.00	694.00
1889	1400.00	34.00	805.00
1890	636.00	35.00	1272.00
1891	716.00	40.00	382.00
1892	881.00	40.00	396.00
1893	823.00		391.00

Comment 1875 RH.3 PITS; 1876 RH.& SPATHOSE & PAINT ORE; 1877
BH.; 1878 PAINT ORE; 1882 WINFORD

Production: Lead	Ore(tons)	Metal(tons)	Value(£)
1846	4.00	3.00	
1848	41.00	29.00	
1849	50.00	41.00	
1852	100.00	70.00	
1856	750.00	500.00	
1857	485.80	351.00	
1858	1000.00	435.00	

135

Lead	Ore(tons)	Metal(tons)	Value(£)
1859	850.00	400.00	
1860	800.00	357.00	
1861	860.00	330.00	
1862	750.00	375.00	
1863	700.00	300.00	
1864	2374.30	667.00	
1865	1050.00	626.50	
1866	1132.00	675.00	
1867	884.00	531.00	
1868	1135.00	606.00	
1869	1537.50	621.10	
1870	1337.00	523.00	
1871	1888.00	632.30	
1872	1322.20	602.90	
1873	752.70	464.50	
1874	1479.10	402.70	
1875	1546.20	454.90	
1876	578.00	301.40	3728.40
1877	452.90	310.50	3514.20
1878	539.20	318.30	3273.90
1879		301.90	4475.60
1880	472.70	112.90	4169.70
1881	363.80	140.80	2343.20
1882	276.00	63.30	799.00
1883	491.00	131.20	1200.00
1884	664.00	178.00	1055.00
1896	550.00	400.00	2200.00
1897	229.00	167.00	2824.00
1898	268.00	214.00	1072.00
1901	1000.00	172.00	2000.00
1902	984.00	187.00	2852.00
1903	200.00	70.00	1072.00
1905	134.00	34.00	386.00
1906	350.00	155.00	1963.00
1907	936.00	345.00	4914.00
1908	576.00	219.00	2677.00

Comment 1846 MENDIP HILLS; 1848-1849 MENDIP HILLS; 1852
MENDIP HILLS; 1856-1859 MENDIP HILLS; 1860-1861 MENDIPS ORE &
SLIMES EST; 1862 MENDIP HILLS; 1863 MENDIP HILLS ORE EST.;
1864-1867 MENDIP HILLS; 1868 MENDIP HILLS EST.; 1869 MENDIP
HILLS PARTLY EST.; 1870-1872 MENDIP HILLS EST; 1873-1884
MENDIP HILLS; 1896 QUARRIES; 1897 OLD HEAPS; 1898 QUARRIES
EST; 1901-1903 QUARRIES EST; 1905-1907 QUARRIES; 1908
QUARRIES ORE EST

SUNDRIES NO.4   0060

Production: Barytes	Ore(tons)	Value(£)
1881	110.00	65.00

136

Arsenic—(Crude and refined, obtained at the Mines), and Arsenical Pyrites.

Name and Situation of Mine.	Owner.	Quantity.	Value at the Mine.
CORNWALL:		Tons. cwts.	£
Botallack, St. Just - (*Arsenical Soot*)	Botallack Mining Co. - - -	78 12	312
Calstock and Danescombe, Calstock (*Arsenical Pyrites*).	Calstock and Danescombe Consolidated Mining Co.	903 4	151
Carn Brea, Redruth (*Arsenical Soot*)	Carn Brea Mining Co. - - -	27 0	81
Drakewalls, Calstock - - (*ditto*)	Drakewalls Tin and Copper Mining Co.-	25 3	143
East Pool, Illogan - - (*ditto*)	East Pool Mining Co. - - -	655 0	4,167
Holmbush, Stoke Climsland (*Refined Arsenic*).	New Holmbush Mining Co., Ltd. -	1,103 0	9,436
Killifreth, Chacewater (*Arsenical Soot*)	Killifreth Mining Co. - - -	14 0	39
Levant, St. Just - - (*ditto*)	Levant Mining Co. - - -	110 0	467
West Wheal Peevor, Redruth - (*ditto*)	West Wheal Peevor Adventurers -	20 0	100
Okel Tor and Cotehele, Calstock (*Refined Arsenic*).	Okel Tor Co., Ltd. - -	551 10	4,400
South Wheal Crofty, Illogan - (*ditto*)	South Wheal Crofty Mining Co. -	156 10	1,071
Tehidy Tin Stream, Illogan (*Arsenical Pyrites*).	Tehidy Tin Stream Works Co. -	10 0	10
Tincroft, Illogan - (*Arsenical Soot*)	Tincroft Mine Adventurers -	69 9	382
Tolgarrick, Tuckingmill - (*ditto*)	John Williams - - -	9 10	34
West Poldice United, Gwennap (*ditto*)	West Poldice United Mining Co. -	87 7	551
West Wheal Seton, Camborne (*ditto*)	West Wheal Seton Adventurers -	226 10	1,401
Wheal Agar, Redruth - - (*ditto*)	Wheal Agar Mining Co.- - -	190 1	1,177
Wheal Arthur Mine Stamps, Calstock (*Arsenical Soot*).	Wheal Arthur Proprietors -	18 0	113
Wheal Comford, Gwennap (*Arsenical Pyrites*).	Wheal Comford and North Tresavean Adventurers.	13 0	22
Wheal Jane, Kea - (*Arsenical Soot*)	Cost Book - - -	5 0	5
Totals - - - - - - -	- - - -	4,272 16	24,062
DEVONSHIRE:			
Bedford United, Tavistock (*Arsenical Pyrites*).	Bedford United Mining Co. -	814 15	936
Belstone, Okehampton - (*ditto*)	Mid-Devon Copper Mining Co., Ltd. -	20 19	24
Devon Great Consols, Tavistock (*Refined Arsenic*).	Devon Great Consols Co., Ltd. - -	3,198 6	25,586
Devon Friendship,Mary Tavy (*Arsenical Soot*).	Devon Friendship Mining Co. -	515 0	3,090
Gawton, Tavistock - (*ditto*)	Gawton Copper Mining Co. -	845 16	5,286
Totals - - - - - - -	- -	5,394 16	34,922
Totals for the United Kingdom - - - - - -	-	9,667 12	58,984